1993 North American Fishing Club

MEMBERS' COOKBOOK

Edited by
Ron Larsen
Colleen Ferguson

Published by the North American Fishing Club
Minnetonka, Minnesota 55343

We would like to thank the following for their help:

NAFC Charter Members, who submitted incredible fish recipes for this year's Members' Cookbook, and for supporting the lifetime sport of fishing by joining the North American Fishing Club. This book is dedicated to those who have to clean, package and store their fish. It also is dedicated to those who cook in a hot kitchen and grill in the great outdoors.

NAFC Staff Members, Publisher Mark LaBarbera, Editor Steve Pennaz, Managing Editor Ron Larsen, Associate Editor Colleen Ferguson, Editorial Assistant Mary Petrie-Terry, Vice President of Product Marketing Mike Vail, Marketing Manager Cal Franklin and Project Coordinator Laura Resnik.

Cover photo contributed by Mark LaBarbera. Book design created by Irene Waldridge of Greyfox Communications. Text chapters authored by Lou Bignami. Inside photos provided by Paul DeMarchi and *North American Fisherman* Editor Steve Pennaz. All illustrations by David Rottinghaus.

*Address reprint requests and
orders for additional books to:*
NAFC Cookbook Editor
P.O. Box 3403
Minnetonka, MN 55343

ISBN 0-914697-50-1
Copyright 1992, North American Fishing Club

The North American Fishing Club offers a line of
fraternal products for members. For information, write:
NAFC, P.O. Box 3408, Minnetonka, MN 55343.

CONTENTS

1993 Members' Cookbook

Everything You Need To Know About Cooking Fish 5
by Steve Pennaz, Executive Director

Why Eat Fish? 11

Safe And Savory 17

Best Preserving Methods 25

Cooking The Catch 33

Recipes 43

    Bass 43

    Bluefish 57

    Bluegill 58

    Catfish 61

    Cod 68

    Crappie 71

    Flounder 76

    Gar 78

    Halibut 79

    Mackerel 82

    Mahi Mahi 83

    Northern 85

    Orange Roughy 89

Perch 90

Redfish 94

Red Mullet 95

Red Snapper 96

Salmon 98

Shark 116

Snook 117

Sole 118

Striper 119

Sturgeon 121

Swordfish 122

Trout 123

Tuna 138

Walleye 140

Weakfish 146

Yellowtail 147

Your Choice 148

Index 191

Contributing Members 197

Everything You Need To Know About Cooking Fish

*I*t was late when we got off the lake, but we didn't want to wait until morning to clean the nine walleyes resting in our livewell. Mark headed to our rented cabin for a couple fillet knives and plastic bags, while I carried the fish to the nearby fish-cleaning shack.

Despite the late hour (past midnight) there were two other anglers in the shack. They had already cleaned their fish and were deep into a discussion on the proper way to freeze fish. (A bizarre topic for the middle of the night I'll admit, but it did highlight the confusion many anglers share about the proper way to store fish.) One of the men had brought an empty half-gallon milk carton, which he planned to fill with a mixture of water and fillets, and then freeze. The other man was holding a couple of gallon-sized plastic bags, obviously planning to freeze his fish in them.

The two men left before Mark arrived with the knives and

bags. When Mark did arrive, he found me chuckling over what had just happened. Then the predictable happened. The two of us got into the very same discussion that the previous two fishermen had. (It must have been the full moon!) Of course, nothing was settled that evening, except the theme for this year's *NAFC Members' Cookbook*.

From Hook To Pan

So what is the best way to freeze fish? Good question— we'll answer it a little later. Here's a tougher one. What are the freezer lives of crappies, salmon and catfish?

Surprisingly, many anglers don't realize that freezer life can vary a great deal depending upon the fish species. This is another question we'll answer later.

Common sense goes a long way when cleaning, storing and cooking fish; however, there are definite ways to ensure the freshness and taste of the fish you save for you and your family.

Of course, in these days of fish-consumption advisories on some waters, it's important to know how to remove a fillet's contaminated portions. We'll cover that, as well as detailing easy ways to remove pesky bones in species such as pike. Next we'll tell you what the best materials are for packaging and freezing fish so you can avoid dehydration (freezer burn) and preserve the taste and texture of the fish you keep for the family table. We'll also discuss the best ways to thaw frozen fish which, if done incorrectly, can lead to spoiled fish under some circumstances.

Cooking Tips

This edition of the *NAFC Members' Cookbook* is chock full of great recipes. To help you make the most of them we've also included a chapter on cooking tips. Some of the tips we mention are how to measure fish quantity per person, how to avoid overcooking (a common problem) and how to improve the taste of your fish when smoking, grilling, broiling, poaching, frying, baking and steaming.

And Dozens Of Great Recipes

Finally, you'll find dozens of great recipes for at least 27 fish species, from bass to walleyes and yellowtail. All of them were provided by your fellow NAFC Members from across the country for you to enjoy. And if you need any proof about their goodness, ask NAFC staff members like Managing Editor Ron Larsen or Associate Editor Colleen Ferguson, who both made it a point to edit and proofread the recipes *after* lunch because they would get hunger pangs if they read them on empty stomachs.

Oh, The Answers!

Which is the best way to freeze fish? Well, both of the men had the right idea. The man who likes to use plastic bags will encounter good success if he removes all of the air in the bag before sealing and freezing. Likewise, the man who uses milk cartons as storage containers will enjoy good eating, plus the added benefit of being able to keep his fish fresh twice as long. And freezer life? Well, nothing lasts forever, even fish stored in a solid block of ice. Plan to store lean fish like perch, crappies and walleyes no more than eight months and fatty fish like lake trout and salmon no more than six months.

I hope you enjoy the latest volume of the *NAFC Members' Cookbook!*

Steve

Steve Pennaz
Executive Director
North American Fishing Club

COOKBOOK ABBREVIATIONS

tsp.	=	teaspoon
T.	=	tablespoon
pt.	=	pint
oz.	=	ounce
lb.	=	pound
pkg.	=	package

MEASUREMENT CONVERSIONS

1 pinch	=	less than ⅛ tsp.
1 tbsp.	=	3 tsp.
2 tbsp.	=	1 oz.
4 tbsp.	=	¼ cup
5 tbsp. + 1 tsp.	=	⅓ cup
8 tbsp.	=	½ cup
10 tbsp. + 2 tsp.	=	⅔ cup
12 tbsp.	=	¾ cup
16 tbsp.	=	1 cup

1 cup	=	8 oz.
1 pint	=	16 oz.
1 quart	=	32 oz.
1 gallon	=	128 oz.

1 cup	=	½ pint
2 cups	=	1 pint
4 cups	=	1 quart
2 pints	=	1 quart
4 pints	=	½ gallon
8 pints	=	1 gallon
4 quarts	=	1 gallon
8 gallons	=	1 bushel

COOKING FISH

Why Eat Fish?

Safe And Savory

Best Preserving Methods

Cooking Methods And Tips

Why Eat Fish?

G astronomes have enjoyed eating fish since before the
days of the Roman Empire when those born into royalty
considered fish to be an aphrodisiac. Scarcity of certain fish
probably enters in here, too. People tend to prize fish like
trout or bass because these fish can be difficult to acquire.
(You could argue, however, that yellow perch offer a more
tasty treat than the usual spillway-model, hatchery rainbow.)

Savings are also cited by the budget-minded who claim
they "break even" by eating the fish they catch. (Anyone
who believes that can easily convince a spouse that a bass
boat is really needed to catch fish.) A more realistic
approach is that fish are a bonus for being able to spend
relaxing days on or near the water.

The health-conscious person concurs with grandma's claim
that "fish is brain food." As often seems the case, grandma
was correct. Fish offer many health benefits.

The Japanese and the Inuits of the arctic eat a lot of fish and enjoy much lower rates of heart disease and other health problems. Worldwide, fish-eating people seem generally healthy, and, as a rule, are less obese than meat-eaters. There are many reasons for this, including lifestyle variations, but the result seems clear: Fish (not apples) may help keep the doctor away.

Even fatty species like lake trout offer only 200 calories per 4-ounce serving. Lean fish such as yellow perch may run 100 calories per 4-ounce serving. This compares with 300 calories for a similar-sized serving of beef or pork.

A single, 4-ounce serving of fish also offers half the protein requirements for an adult in an 85- to 90-percent digestible package which helps the young, the old and the infirm. Best of all, fish fat is mostly polyunsaturated; it won't clog your arteries.

Cholesterol levels in fish run low, too. Even a fatty fish like albacore has only about 60 milligrams of cholesterol per 4-ounce serving. (Eggs may have 550 milligrams each!)

However, the current "hot button" for eating fish is the Omega-3, long-chain fatty acids that seem to be associated with lower cholesterol and triglyceride levels, helping to mitigate the severity of such health problems as migraine headaches or arthritis.

Luring Reluctant Fish-Eaters

Even though they know fish are good for them, reluctant fish-eaters need their special reservations addressed directly. A U.S. Advisory Committee nationwide survey was conducted to find the reasons why people eat less fish than meat. The following statistics resulted:

- 26 percent disliked bones
- 20 percent weren't in the habit of buying fish
- 19 percent bought fish, but only on Friday
- 13 percent could not find quality fish
- 12 percent disliked cleaning fish
- 7 percent thought buying fish was too expensive
- 3 percent didn't know how to prepare fish

First, serve boneless fillets.

Second, catch your own.

Third, eat fish as soon as possible after it's caught. For example, if you go on a fishing excursion over the weekend,

Fats And Figures (4-Ounce Servings)

	Calories	Omega-3s gms	Cholesterol mg
Channel Catfish	125	0.1	111
Cod	85	0.2	55
Halibut	120	0.5	40
Perch, Yellow	100	0.2	90
Pike, Northern	95	0.1	45
Salmon, Chinook	200	2.0	70
Salmon, Silver	145	1.9	39
Trout, Brook	115	0.3	68
Trout, Lake	175	1.5	60
Trout, Rainbow	140	0.5	50
Walleye	95	0.2	85
Whitefish, Lake	170	0.8	65

This chart provides some dietary information for the health-conscious fish-eater. Although not all fish species are listed, these popular ones will help when comparing.

eat the fish you catch on Sunday night or Monday.

Fourth, ensure the quality of fish by depending upon your own skills on the lake and in the kitchen.

Fifth, only clean fish for your own use or for use in a group meal. In other words, don't clean fish that will be given away.

Sixth, never let your friends and relatives know how much your "free" fish really cost, including the cost of boats, gear, gas and tackle.

Seventh, follow tried-and-recommended recipes such as the ones in this *NAFC Members' Cookbook*, and you won't go wrong.

Eat The Best

Euell Gibbons, the gleaner's guru, put it best in his classic, *Stalking The Blue-Eyed Scallop*, when he noted, "... I have found that many of the neglected little fish, when skillfully prepared, are much better eating than the trophy-sized rarities sought by the Simon-pure sportsman." Even though he spoke of saltwater fish, the same is true of freshwater fish.

Most experts agree that yellow perch, bluegills or brook trout rank near the top of the taste list. In the trout family, a 6- to 9-inch brookie from a cold-water stream ranks first. Other things being equal, fish from streams taste better than the same species from lakes—this seems to be a matter of texture as much as taste.

Yellow perch taken through the ice, or bluegills taken from a clear creek are difficult to beat in taste. This isn't to say gamefish such as steelhead or walleyes don't taste great. Instead, such fish that offer a perfect fight seem more valuable contributing to the gene pool than temporarily gracing a platter.

Catching "mini"-fish from ponds or streams seems to make a positive impact on the piscatorial environment. Panfish and brook trout tend to stunt if not harvested. We've all seen schools of mature 4- or 5-inch bluegills, or lakes with bright brookies that are one-third head. Some states, Idaho for example, recognize this with a 10-brookie limit in addition to six other trout. Most states offer liberal or open panfish limits so you can bring home all the fish you need to fill the freezer.

Catch mini-fish and you're guaranteed all the action you can handle. Someone once said, "If bluegills were as big as bass, we'd need tuna-weight tackle." Use an ultra-light outfit and not more than 2-pound test, and you've put the sport back into "sportfishing."

Given a short-bladed, flexible fillet knife and a minimum amount of effort, mini-fish offer the best possible taste and texture. Anyone who has eaten large and small lake trout won't be surprised to hear smaller fish are always more tasty. Sure, you may only get a bite-sized fillet from each side of the body of a 5-inch bluegill, but these fish will fillet fast. You won't have to worry about saving every last scrap of meat. Such tiny fillets or small, soft fish, such as trout, cook as fast as you can flip them in a skillet.

Eating the smaller fish helps ensure safety.Small, young fish contain lower levels of PCBs, mercury and the other dubious delights of the industrial world that find their way

Mini-fish from cold water taste fantastic. Catching bluegills through the ice, for example, helps ensure a delicious, savory meal later.

into our waters. Young fish have had less time to absorb such contaminants. Big predators, like muskies or pike, concentrate chemicals from other fish over a longer period of time.

Release The Best

Big fish, especially big breeding females that are almost always the largest of their species, deserve a chance to reproduce. This is the reason for size and slot limits, as well as voluntary catch-and-release fishing.

Other things being equal, big females simply produce more eggs. For example, a big sturgeon might release 10 or more times the eggs of a smaller fish in its first fertile season. Therefore, fishermen should treasure such fish and release them with care. Even the case for keeping trophy fish seems weak when you consider the quality of fiberglass mounts requiring only a good photo, and length and girth measurements. It's easy to compute weight from these figures, and the result of a released fish is a future catch.

Catch 'Em Quick

However, it's certainly better for the fish to be taken quickly on adequate tackle and carefully released where caught than to be either exhausted on ultra-light, or toted around in a livewell all day before being released back at the ramp.

Switch Rather Than Fight

While catch-and-release fishing works for many fishermen, some of the most experienced anglers take this a step further. When big trout, for example, are easy to catch, a skilled angler will most likely move to another species to maximize the challenge.

Even a 5-percent loss ratio on release can clean out heavily fished areas such as prime Western trout streams. If several thousand fishermen went through such a stream for a summer (which is not uncommon on popular waters), you would radically reduce the size and number of fish even if none were kept.

Happily, the problem solves itself. Experienced and skilled fishermen no longer seem to concentrate on catching a limit, a big fish, a limit of big fish and a record. Instead they concentrate on tough-to-catch fish. Professionals don't need to sort through 20 salmon to find a 70-pound trophy. Professional angler Homer Circle once said, "I'd rather catch a batch of bluegills on a fly rod than a trophy trout." Such long-time, skilled fishermen rarely see the need to catch bass off nests or salmon off spawning redds. The challenge simply isn't there. Instead, they might go to ultra-light tackle and load their freezers with panfish that, in most parts of the country, stunt because of overpopulations due to limited harvests.

Common sense suggests that the angler who limits his take of big fish and keeps only what he can eat ensures the maximum sustained fishing pleasure for everyone.

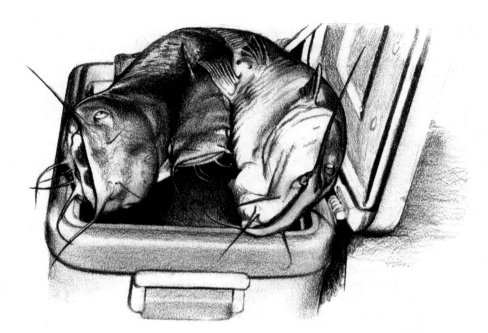

Safe And Savory

Periodic reports about contaminated waters or fish raise
the issue of safely eating fish. However, most of these
reports fade with time, as did "cancer-berry reports" that
removed a favorite sauce from Thanksgiving tables years
ago. Today, the public's view on safely eating fish seems to
vary with the latest report. Some would have us pass through
nature in hermetically sealed rubber suits; others take
excessive risks. Following the advice of a Greek motto,
"moderation in all things," and making a phone call to the
local health department should cover the bases.

It's possible that eating pounds of fish taken from a toxic
waste pond could turn up your toes. It's more likely,
however, that you could be struck and killed by lightning.
Thus, only the most compulsive fish-eaters whose daily menu
is limited to a single fish species and a specific body of
water could jeopardize their health in this way.

The chance of harming your health is apparently greatest with raw fish and shellfish. Young children and expectant mothers should limit their intake of fish from questionable waters. However, according to acute disease estimates (not just those reported), the safest source of muscle protein available on a weight-consumed basis is fish.

Hook To Home

Safe and savory fish deserve the best care, and the warmer the weather the more care is needed! Fresh fish always taste better. In the very best Chinese restaurants, patrons choose their meals from live tanks.

If not crowded, small fish will remain lively in an aerated livewell or in a mesh bag hanging over the boat's side. (Remove dead fish immediately.) Big fish should be hit on the head so they don't bruise themselves on the boat.

After they are eviscerated or filleted, place meat on a layer of crushed ice in a cooler. If you have no crushed ice, break up block ice and add a little water to make a slush. Fish keep in crushed ice or slush for two or three days. On longer trips you can keep fish cool in a mixture of one pound salt to 20 pounds ice. Fish keep in this mix for up to a week. Both methods require draining excess liquid.

If you can't tote an ice chest, fill an inexpensive mesh bag with wet leaves, grass or moss which will keep fish fresh. Avoid rubberized fabric "fish poachers" on vests that rarely improve the taste or texture of your catch. On longer trips where nights are cold, you can hang eviscerated fish on a line to chill. Make sure the line is out of reach of raccoons and bears. Take your fish in before sunup, wrap them in layered newspaper and put them in a plastic bag. Insert the bag into a sleeping bag. Roll up the bag and store it out of the sun. Repeat this procedure each day.

Cut-Ups Considered

Eviscerating fish as soon as they are caught starts the cooling process. So does filleting if you place the fillets in sealed plastic bags tucked into crushed ice. The decision depends upon personal preference, available time and intended use.

Eviscerating fish while leaving the skin and head on reduces the loss of natural juices during storage and

Preparing Fish For Freezer

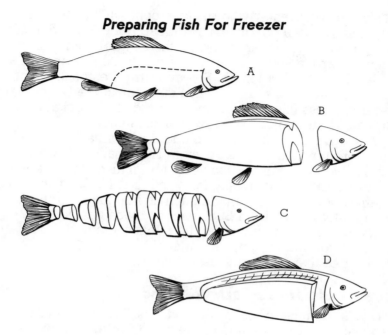

There are various ways to prepare your fish for the freezer. Eviscerating comes first (A). Then, you can leave the fish whole (B), or you can steak (C) or fillet (D) it, depending upon your preference.

cooking. Scaling fresh fish is better than prying off stiff, dry scales later; filleting fish in the field saves time and mess at home. (Skinless fillets also eliminate the need to scale fish.)

Use either the vent-to-gill-slit method in which the throat connection is cut so the whole innards can be pulled out intact, or, for round fish, go with the standard system in which the gills and guts are removed from the body cavity. With flat fish, such as bluegills, you should chop the heads off at an angle to remove the gills. In all cases remember to remove the dark kidney, or bloodline, that runs along the backbone's gut-side. A spoon or dull table knife can be used to scrape the kidney out. (On big fish, such as lake trout, you need to slit the pouch, too.)

Filleting Fast

Fish fillets are easier to cook, conserve storage space and

satisfy the picky eater who dislikes bones. Filleting fish seems easy when conditions are ideal, but can be difficult with improper equipment and methods. Start with a firm cutting board, a sharp knife with a comfortable grip and a blade of the correct length. Select a firm, fresh fish which has been wiped dry, and always cut against the bone. If you prefer skinless fillets, cut away from the skin. Package the leftovers for tidy disposal or further cleaning.

A sharp fillet knife with a blade a bit longer than the fish's depth makes the task easier. The smaller of two popular wooden-handled knives with Finnish-steel blades like Normark's works nicely for small fish. Larger fish would require a longer, stiffer blade such as that found in the folding fillet knives from Buck Knives. Because the knife choice depends greatly upon the filleting method, it's important for you to know about each method. The procedures that follow are used worldwide.

Three Cuts/Three Parts Rib Chop

This is the most popular method. You begin by making a diagonal cut along the line of the ribs from the top of the fish to the bottom. The blade is then turned toward the tail and the fillet sawed off as the knife crunches through the backbone's ribs. Discard the entrails and belly; trim the belly meat. Then the ribs are pared and, if you like, the skin is removed by running the fillet knife next to it. This method is easy, basic and messy.

Rib-Lift Fillets

This method also begins with the basic diagonal cut. However, a cut is made back toward the tail by pressing the knife's side against the backbone and dorsal fin as the knife tip bounces along the ribs without cutting them. This last step depends more on feel than sight. You can get the "feel" by lightly running a knife point over a closed zipper.

Reverse the blade edge so it faces the tail and stick the knife through the fish next to the backbone, just behind the vent. Using the backbone as a blade rest, cut the tail-end of the fillet free. Then free the other end of the fillet by running the knife blade over the ribs toward the belly. Flop the fish over so the other fillet can be done in the same way. If you like skinless fillets or don't want to scale the fish, trim around the fins and belly and strip off the skin by running the knife under it with the fillet's skin-side down.

Innards stay inside the rib cage and can easily be disposed along with the skin. (This is also a good approach for leaving skin on fillets.) The method's disadvantage is it's difficult to pin down the fillets while you're stripping the skin.

Flip-Flop Filleting

Flip-flop filleting differs from the rib-lift method after you have bounced your knife point along the ribs. At the back end of the ribs, the knife punches down and through the skin, coming out just behind the vent. With the knife pressed against the backbone to minimize waste, the fish is cut down to the tail, but not through its skin. Then remove the knife and use it to "peel" the fillet off the ribs. When the fillet is freed except where it is still attached at the tail, flip it over onto the board. The direction of the knife's blade is then reversed. Using the unfilleted side of the fish as a handle, separate the fillet from the skin as the flexible blade puts lateral pressure on the skin. (When you're trimming off the skin, it helps to move the fillet to the board's edge. This provides clearance for the knife handle so that the blade will stay flat, minimizing waste.) The process is then repeated on the other side of the fish. The result should be two skinless fillets and a body, innards intact, with the cut-off skin still attached, ready for disposal. Don't worry if you accidentally slice off a fillet with its skin. It's easy to simply separate the fillet from the skin, with the fillet skin-side down as in the previous method.

Beware The Y-Bone

Fillets with the famous Y-bone lurking just above the ribs require a couple more cuts after the fillet has been freed from the fish on the board. First, slice off the thin meat strip above the Y-bone, using the Y-bone as a guide. The second cut separates the larger lower meat section from over the ribs. What's left is the triangular Y-bone and a small amount of meat within the Y that's good for stock or grinding.

Filleting Fish

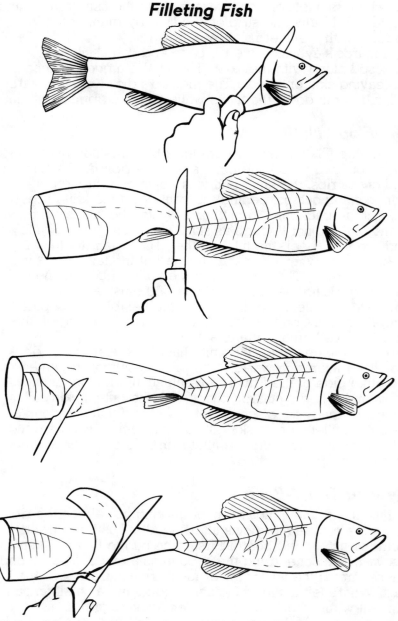

Filleting fish is the most popular method when preparing for freezing or cooking. You need a sharp knife and a steady hand. Here, the filleting process is illustrated for you step by step.

The Catfish Connection

Look ugly, clean tough and eat good. This describes these scaleless whiskerfish. The traditional catfish-cleaning method is very messy. Pliers are used to skin the cat while its held in place with various contraptions. If you use a very sharp knife or a single-edged razor blade to cut the skin along both sides of dorsal fins, either the rib-lift or flip-flop method will work with small catfish. The basic, three-cut method works well with an electric fillet knife. Big catfish should be steaked.

Lifting Lateral Lines

Lateral lines in fish vary in width and thickness. (They are the dark flesh that usually runs through the middle of the fillet.) They also collect contaminants and are strong tasting. Carp from cool water are quite edible when poached if the lateral line is removed, assuming you've eliminated the Y-bones. You can imagine the taste of most bass, pike and saltwater species if the lateral line is carefully removed with an extremely sharp knife. Don't bother to do this with salmon or trout; their lateral lines don't taste strong.

Partial Filleting

Many anglers cut the flesh on salmon and other large fish from behind the gills to the vent into "steaks." Then they fillet the tails with the flip-flop or rib-lift method. With very large fish, it's sometimes necessary to cut fillets up into "half steaks" so the meat will cook thoroughly. If fillets vary more than 50 percent in thickness, trim them!

The Nose Knows Fresh Fish

Specialty fish markets may charge a bit more, but their fish are often more fresh. Entering a good fish market, you can immediately tell its overall quality by the smell. Fresh fish smell like an ocean breeze. If a market or fish package smells like a mudflat at low tide, move on.

Quality fish markets look good, too. Fish are carefully displayed on crushed ice. It helps to pick up your selection with both hands so the fillets or steaks won't tear.

It's worth noting that the Chinese, who are compulsive

about fresh foods, simply won't buy fish that are not "in the round." Fish in the round, or drawn, let you look at the eye, which should be bright and slightly bulging with—in most species except salmon—dark corneas. Gills must be bright red and moist, not dark or sticky.

Dressed fish without heads require a different test. If you lightly press the flesh, it should spring back without leaving an indention.

Fillets and steaks should be firm without dark spots. Dark spots indicate rough handling; browning at the edges indicates spoiling. As with packaged fish, avoid any package with liquid in the bottom!

The worst possible ways to buy fish are breaded and in plastic trays covered with plastic wrap at the supermarket. You can't see the fish you're buying and you don't know what's in the coating. Even with nude fish you can't see the other side of the fish. Is that side ever better looking?

If you must buy fish packed in plastic trays, try the "fickle finger" test. Run your finger along the tray's bottom. Then smell your finger. If it smells "fishy," try another tray.

Wherever you buy fish, ask about sulfites. Some markets and packers use sulfites to improve the looks and storage time of fish. Sulfite allergies can cause problems. Phosphate dips, usually under 5 percent, are also used. While not yet considered harmful, dips at the legally allowed 10 percent maximum concentration can make fish taste rather soapy.

Freezer And Refrigerator Factors

Frozen fish that are properly thawed in the market can offer decent value. However, freshly thawed fish in supermarket display cases often seem soft. In most cases, you're better off buying frozen fish if solidly frozen and stored at below 10 degrees F. In any case, never hold thawed fish for more than 24 hours.

Try to eat fish the same day you buy it. Also keep the fish chilled from market to stove. If you are not going home immediately from the market, ask the cashier or bagger to seal your fish in a plastic bag inside an outer bag filled with crushed ice.

Best Preserving Methods

*T*ossing fish into the freezer without much thought is easy; however, investing some time in fish preparation, quick freezing and storage at a temperature below zero F will help ensure fresh taste and a succulent texture. Preparation starts immediately after catching the fish. It continues at home with acidic dips, decent wrapping and methods that minimize oxidation and dehydration. Considering proper portion sizes and using a good label system should result in a year's worth of fine fish eating.

Freeze It Fast

Quick freezing minimizes the size of internal ice crystals in frozen fish. (Big crystals puncture cell walls allowing succulent juices to escape.) Quick freezing also reduces bacteria and enzyme action which occurs before the fish freezes completely. Speed is especially important when freezing fatty fish. This is because most of their moisture is in unsaturated oils. These oils freeze at a lower temperature than water. When slowly freezing, these oils can leak out of cells ruptured by ice crystals and cause a rancid taste.

You should never freeze more than 2 pounds of fish per cubic foot of freezer space at one time. Placing unfrozen fish packages on freezer coils in the coldest part of the freezer speeds freezing, too. Air spaces around the fish packages also helps.

After your fish packages freeze, stack them tightly together. This increases space in your freezer and decreases your operating cost. (The fuller the freezer, the smaller the air volume that must be cooled each time the freezer opens.)

Fail Safe

A full freezer's contents may stay frozen for 48 hours in a power outage; a half-full freezer would thaw in 24 hours. In an emergency, 25 pounds of dry ice per cubic foot of freezer space placed on top of foods can extend this period up to three days or more.

Freezer temperature is quite critical. Zero is 32 degrees below freezing. Even if you open and close your freezer's door often, your fish will stay below the critical, 10-degree temperature mark (indicated in Chapter 2). Freeze fish at zero for at least 72 hours and you will eliminate parasite problems, too.

If your freezer is set above zero, your fish preservation time is reduced by two months. This is also true with the typical refrigerator's freezer compartment which should be used only as a temporary holding area for foods consumed within the month. An inexpensive freezer thermometer or the "ice cream test" can help monitor freezer temperatures. If ice cream from the freezer is difficult to scoop, do not worry. Also freezer frost will reduce storage time for fish. This is because it raises the storage temperature. Freezers should be defrosted every six months or whenever a ½-inch-thick frost layer forms.

Avoiding Oxidation And Dehydration

Experts agree that 85 percent of problems with home-frozen foods relate to inadequate packaging. Fifteen percent result from poor initial quality, preparation errors and slow freezing. Even a short freeze can reduce fish quality if wrapping isn't done correctly.

First, there must be a moisture/vapor-proof barrier between your fish and the freezer. Otherwise, dehydration, or freezer burn, can discolor fish as moisture migrates from fish flesh out into the freezer. Oxidation works the opposite way. It's caused when oxygen leaks into the fish and causes rancidity by changing the fat-containing cells in your fish. This is the reason fatty fish don't keep as long as lean fish. The easy way to bar both transfers is with impermeable wraps or ice-barrier systems.

Wild Wraps

Wrapping is the most popular freeze-storage approach. Don't use just any wrapping material. Look for wraps that are both vapor-proof and oxygen resistant. The best wraps are flexible enough to fold into a tight package and strong enough to prevent possible damage from fish spines. When in doubt, double wrap!

Worthwhile wraps start with fish hugging, heavy-duty, freezer-weight foils. Transparent clingwraps with heavy, puncture-proof outer layers help prevent problems. Coated and laminated wrapping papers offer good, outer layers. They are also decent double-wraps for those who don't use clinging inner layers.

Two wrapping methods work best. Drugstore wraps are similar to common-wraps used for gifts. However, the double or triple fold is added to prevent moisture leaks along the seam. Butcher wraps start with fish on the corner of a rather large piece of paper. The fish are rolled toward the opposite corner of the paper and, with each revolution, turned 90 degrees. The result is several layers of protective paper. Both wrap systems work either alone, in double layers or as an outer layer over films and foils. (The glossy, coated or laminated side is the inside surface.) Butchers often sell industrial-sized rolls of film, foil and paper wraps at considerable savings over supermarket prices.

Butcher's Wrap

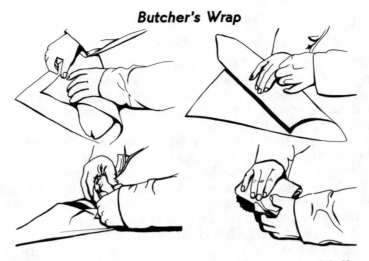

The butcher wrap is an extremely popular method for packaging fish. You place the fish on the corner of the paper and roll it toward the opposite side, turning 90 degrees with each revolution.

Heat Sealers

Heat-sealed film bags produced from rolls of plastic tubing by popular vacuum baggers work well, too. Durability depends upon the wrap's thickness, the way the vacuum sealer exhausts air from the package and the seal quality. Weight seems to be a good guide for durability, and more expensive films can, according to some sealer manufacturers, be downsized and reused a second time. (An outer layer of protective paper wrap over the heat-seal bag reduces punctures and freezer burn.)

Bag It: The Plastic Solution

Sealable plastic bags work well if all air is expelled from the bag before it is closed. The easy way to do this is to submerge the filled bag almost completely in water, pushing any air out. You can also water-pack fish in bags; ice layers reduce oxidation and dehydration. Place water-filled bags in boxes or other containers to freeze. Then remove the bags; they will stack tightly.

Open-this-end bags from the rolls in the supermarket vegetable section offer a budget bag choice. Even though you need an outer, protective paper layer, these bags seal well and cling tightly to odd fish shapes.

Plastic, Glass And Other Containers

Plastic tubs and other commercial containers work well for precooked dishes and fish frozen in water packs. Glass does not work well with water-packs: It breaks! However, jars with screw-top lids protect while allowing you to see small, whole smoked fish like trout.

Plastic-lined bags, plastic tubing and many other options work, too. Some anglers save butter tubs for fillets or small fish. Fast-food and half-gallon soda containers can be used, as well as gallon-sized plastic containers for big families.

Cartons Considered

Plastic-coated paper milk cartons (all sizes) offer a cheap, convenient solution to freeze-wrapping. Freeze small whole fish, steaks, fillets or fillet parts in the appropriate-sized, water-filled carton, leaving an inch at the top for ice expansion. Then freeze the cartons, making sure no fish is exposed to air. (Add extra water if needed.) Then fold down the top and tape or staple it shut. This process will effectively double the freezer life of your fish. Best of all, when you stack frozen cartons in the freezer there is no wasted air space. Therefore, you decrease operating costs.

Ice Glaze Methods

Large, whole fish require special methods. First, place a trophy-sized fish on a sheet of clingwrap or waxed paper. Then place the fish on your freezer's coldest surface. Prepare a large pan of extremely cold water or one of the dips mentioned below. When the fish surface starts to freeze, plunge the entire fish into the liquid and return to the freezer. Repeat this process until a ¼-inch-thick ice glaze forms. This will keep for two weeks. For longer storage, wrap the fish in moisture-barrier paper or restore the ice layer with periodic recoatings via the liquid bath.

Glazes

Brine dips work well with lean fish like yellow perch. Use ½ cup non-iodized salt per quart of water. Dip fish in the solution and continue with the ice bath or wrap methods.

Acid dips work best for fatty fish like lake trout. (Ascorbic acid is an anti-oxidant that reduces the chance of a rancid taste.) These dips seem common in the commercial fishing industry and are quite safe. A solution of two tablespoons ascorbic acid to a quart of water (follow directions on packages available at most drugstores and canning centers) works well with a 30-second dip, drain, wrap and seal approach.

Gelatin and lemon juice glaze, a variation of acid dip that builds a thicker coat faster than ascorbic acid, starts with 1 cup boiling water and ¼ cup bottled lemon juice. Then a package of unflavored gelatin is dissolved in ½ cup water and added to the boiling mix cooled to room temperature. At this point, the dip is ready to use.

Proper Portions

Don't let a fine mess of fish tempt you into "portly portions." You can always open another package. Families can use larger packages. It's not easy trying to saw off three salmon steaks from a 30-pound frozen fish! One thing seems certain: Large, whole fish are too big for anything except holiday buffets!

Labels And Logs

When using milk cartons, punch codes into the carton top with a hole punch for different species, serving numbers and the date. Or you can use different carton brands (or types) for different species.

Creating a log of freezer contents helps organize your meal planning and prevents spoilage. Also, conducting periodic freezer audits when defrosting helps.

Thawing Frozen Fish

Because bacteria flourish at warm temperatures, thawing fish at room temperature is not a good idea. Several other methods work. Fish frozen in ice blocks can be freed from the ice under cold running water, then refrigerated for 24 hours to thaw gradually. (Make sure to set the fish on a rack

Species Table

Lean (less than 2 percent fat):

freshwater bass	crappie	perch	shark
black sea bass	flounder	pickerel	skate
black drum	grouper	redfish	sole
bluegill	halibut	redsnapper	walleye
burbot	northern pike	rockfish	yellow perch
cod (not hake/whiting)			

Medium (2 to 6 percent fat):

buffalo	hake/whiting	sea trout	sturgeon
carp	muskie	smelt	swordfish
catfish	sauger	striped bass	

Fatty (over 6 percent fat):

bluefish	salmon	sardines	tuna
butterfish	smelt	shad	yellowtail
mahi mahi	salmon	trout	

Lean fish work best with rich butter sauces; however, they require extra basting. Medium fish taste great baked or broiled with mayonnaise-based sauces. And fatty fish are tops for broiling and smoking sans sauces.

over a plate so they don't sit in water.) Another method is to put fish in a waterproof bag in the morning and submerge the bag in a bowl of cold water in the refrigerator. The fish will have thawed in 8 to 10 hours—just in time for dinner!

If in a hurry, you can thaw fish in the microwave. Wash fish out of their ice block first or they will cook during the ice-melt. (Times will vary with the microwave.) On a 50 percent, or "thaw" setting, three to five minutes normally will thaw small whole fish, fillets and steaks. Remove the fish before the thickest part is completely thawed. Then drain the fish and cook; or, cover it and refrigerate.

Frozen Isn't Forever

Nothing keeps forever. A year is tops for lean fish frozen in ice blocks, carefully wrapped with vapor-barrier paper and maintained at zero F. Eight months seems average for lean fish; six months for fatty fish. Fillets and steaks don't keep as long as whole fish.

When fish start to reach their labeled expiration dates, use them (or any freezer-burned fish) for fish stocks. While their taste may not equal fresh fish, they can be used for stock as long as they pass the usual nose test for freshness.

The fat content, flesh color, taste and texture vary within a given species depending on water type, time of year and other factors.

Other Preservation Methods

Canning preserves fish for over a year. It works well for fatty species, such as salmon or trout. It's also a good choice for pike, shad or carp because the small, difficult-to-remove Y-bones soften while canning. Badly sealed jars can be lethal, however, and must be disposed of as soon as possible. Please follow canning instructions carefully.

Smoked trout, salmon, shad or sturgeon deserve their gourmet status. Homemade and commercial smokers work well. The key is a low, controlled temperature resulting from a regulated heat source that will heat apple and other fruitwood chips or sawdust to smoldering. Freeze or refrigerate fish after smoking.

Dried fish is common in tropical climates. It's good if you don't mind a strong taste and chewy consistency; however, it's not recommended in areas of moderate to hot temperatures or high humidity.

Fish were once layered in rock salt and lasted for several months. Most salted fish are now cooked in liquids or reconstituted in liquids before being cooked.

When refrigerating fish, four days seems to be the limit. Put fish on an ice bed and drain daily. Steaks and fillets should be stored in ice bags or covered and placed on the bottom, coldest tray.

For pickling, soak bite-sized chunks of boned fish in a soft-water brine solution with pickling salt and refrigerate overnight. Drain and rinse. Replace fish in bowl, cover with distilled white vinegar and refrigerate overnight. Put pickled fish in container and cover with your favorite cooled pickling solution. Refrigerate a week before serving. This will keep for about five weeks in the refrigerator.

Cooking The Catch

Overcooking has ruined more fish than water pollution. Unlike red meat, fish meat does not become tender with increased cooking. As a general cooking rule, fresh fish meat takes about 10 minutes per inch of thickness at the thickest point; frozen meat takes 20 minutes. Stuffed dishes with many ingredients will require different cooking times.

Whole fish or large fillets can present problems because of varied thicknesses. Slicing big fish into steaks helps avoid many of these problems. Otherwise, the thin tail section cooks faster than the thick shoulder sections.

Canadian guides spit whole fish heads-down over campfires so the thickest parts receive the most heat. Given a large pan, you can place fish so that their thickest parts are over the hot burners. Also, some grills tilt, making it possible to brace broiler pans so that the tail sections are farther from the heat, allowing them to cook more slowly than the thicker parts. (You can achieve the same result on a charcoal grill by separating the briquettes a bit more under the tail-ends.)

Because fish rarely come in uniform sizes, you need some skill and luck. Cooking bigger fish in the pans for a while before adding the small fish helps ensure a hot, properly cooked meal.

Fork Testing

The easiest way to determine if the fish is done is by looking. Uncooked fish meat appears translucent; cooked fish opaque. A small slit at the fish's thickest part or two forks inserted at the fish's median line will help you see. When in doubt, undercook. Fish will continue to cook when removed from pot or pan. You can always return undercooked fish to the fire. Even smothering the meat in sauce won't work with overcooked fish!

Portions

Most recipes feed four to six adults, three hungry anglers or one teenager. Main courses that are rich in taste with delicious sauces and many side dishes suggest servings as small as the 4-ounce standard used for computing calories. However, 6- to 8-ounce servings seem more appropriate for most appetites.

You might offer 10- or 12-ounce servings with whole, head-on, fish like trout or crappies. When you're serving fish steaks, 5 ounces should be plenty. Of course, recipes that permit cooking extra servings for use in making fish balls, fish cakes and other quick dishes will save the chef time in future meal preparation.

Grilling And Barbecuing

Grilling began when a savvy cave-dweller stuck a salmon on a green stick over a fire. Salmon bones found in French caves date back to 25,000 B.C., and Columbia River site discoveries go back to 10,000 B.C. Salmon and fatty fish, like trout, still grill well if you control the heat and the distance between fish and flame. Lean fish cook reasonably well with dedicated basting. Cooking times follow the usual 10-minutes-per-inch formula, but you need to turn fish about two-thirds of the way through because the first side continues to cook after it's flipped.

Even though you can grill fish head-down on a green stick over a campfire, a specialized grill works much better. Grills come in all different types including cheap, yet effective hibachis with adjustable grill surfaces, Turkish grills with vertical charcoal containers and the popular gas grills.

No grill completely solves the "skin stick" problem. Meat from delicate fish tends to separate if not tenderly turned on a well-lubricated grill. Therefore, some cooks grill whole fish with the heads on to reduce the chance of sticking. Cooking the fish with its head on also helps retain the fish's juices. Fish also are set on aluminum foil or cooked in foil envelopes. A special grill basket works even better; it holds fish firmly so they turn over easily. Baskets also allow you to layer your fish with fresh dill, thyme or basil. As these spices dry, char and smoke, their taste permeates the fish.

Outdoor grilling is a popular method for preparing fish. There are three basic types of grills: the hibachi, gas and charcoal. All produce a tasty fish meal.

Temperature is also very important: Wait until the charcoal is quite gray. Space charcoal blocks an inch or two apart from each other. Raise your grill's adjustable rack about 4 or 5 inches to improve results.

Broiling

Urban indoor grilling's main advantage over outdoor grilling is that its heat source is above the fish. This prevents basting liquids from draining away. This system works well for fatty fish, as well as basted lean fish. You can also add boiling stock to the pan under the basting rack so that fish will steam while grilling.

On most conventional ovens, the broil setting is a bit hot when your grill rack is in the top slot; it's also a bit cool when placed in the next slot. You may need to slip an inverted cookie sheet under your grill pan to set the height exactly. Gas and electric grills work differently. Gas grills are intermittent; electric grills are not. Therefore, close the door on gas range ovens; leave it slightly open on electric ovens.

Pan-Frying And Sauteing

The classic rule, "if you can smell it, your fish is probably too hot" applies when pan-frying and sauteing. Pan-frying works best with small, whole lean fish such as panfish or black bass, and moderately well with small salmon or trout. Use only minimal oil to keep your fish from sticking, adding extra oil only as needed. (Allow time for replacement oil to reach correct temperature before adding fish.) A coating of seasoned flour also helps keep fish from sticking. If the oil is cold or the fish are crowded, they will be soggy.

For a light breading, fish can be coated with pancake mix. Sauteing fish in barely brown butter offers a delicious result, especially with delicate fish such as 6- to 8-inch trout or panfish. The fish cook as the skin crisps. Drizzle lemon juice over the fish when done. Whisk a rich sauce for 30 seconds and pour it over your fish.

Oven-Frying

This is a great way to cook many small panfish at one time without smelling up the house. Fillets that are less than an

When panfrying your "catch of the day," it is extremely important not to crowd the fillets in the pan. If you do not allow enough space between them, they will most likely turn out soggy.

inch thick cook more evenly than whole fish or steaks. As with pan-frying, don't crowd fish.

Set your oven to 425 degrees. Pour just enough oil into your pans to cover the bottom and heat the oil for about five minutes. Pat-dry your fish so they don't splatter. Smother fish with your favorite coating and place fillets in the pan, turning once to coat both sides with oil. Then return the pan to the oven for about 10 minutes.

Deep-Fat Frying

Southerners know that deep-fat frying in a big pot of hot vegetable oil produces the most panfish per hour with the least effort. A batter crust and very quick cooking ensure golden brown and moist results. Fortunately, since the fish are submerged, cooking time is five minutes per pound if you keep your vegetable oil at 375 degrees.

If you don't have a deep-fat fryer, a deep electric skillet works reasonably well. A Dutch oven also works on top of the stove if you add a thermometer to ensure even temperatures. As always, a maximum amount of oil and a minimum number of fish pieces improve results. Too many fish at a time get soggy when the oil cools. So cook only a few fish until they are golden brown. Then add more oil, allowing the temperature to rise before adding more fish.

Dip the dry fish (wet fish won't hold batter) into your favorite batter. Beer batters, pancake mixes and "secret formulas" all work if their textures don't result in a thick crust on the fish. A very large bamboo and brass mesh scoop, which can be found at Chinese cooking supply houses, is the best tool for removing cooked fish and stray cooked batter.

Baking

Baking works well for fillets and steaks and wonderfully well for large chunks or whole fish like pike, salmon or steelhead. Leave the head and skin on to help retain natural juices. Oily fish should be raised above the pan with a rack. Lean fish require basting with pan juices. Most baked fish look best if basted with butter or pan juices and browned a bit under the broiler.

Your favorite butter-basted stuffings, like those used with turkeys, go well with fish. Dry stuffings, such as corn bread, taste great with oily fish. Do allow a little extra cooking time in addition to the usual 12 minutes per pound for stuffed fish.

Removing whole baked fish from the pan can be difficult. To solve this problem, fish can be baked on aluminum foil or racks from fish steamers. Some ovenware can both cook and present baked fish. Just use a bulb baster to remove juices needed for sauce.

Microwaving

When microwaving fish, you will obtain the best results when the fish is taken out just before it flakes. Use 100 percent power for lean fish; 50 percent (or thaw) for fatty fish. Brush fish with lime or lemon juice, melted margarine or butter before putting it in the microwave. Cover it with a sheet of waxed paper and cook it for half the expected cooking time. Then rearrange the fish so the less-cooked parts are on the outside and continue cooking. Cooking times will run less than the classic 10-minutes-per-inch but will vary depending upon the microwave, number of fish and other factors.

Poaching And Fish-Boiling

Cooking fish in hot liquid works best with oily fish like salmon, trout and steelhead. It also offers both an easy base for sauces and stocks and the chance to enhance the flavor without adding calories.

Poaching fish in simmering liquid enriched with vegetables and seasonings also works well when you're uncertain of the exact time you'll be eating. Poaching a few minutes beyond the usual 10-minutes-per-inch of thickness formula won't ruin the result.

Because poaching is done best with whole fish with heads left on, you should consider using a specialized long pan. Getting the fish out of the poaching liquid whole can be difficult, but this problem is solved with rack inserts in specialized fish poachers. Long spatulas and a custom-cut rack made from an old oven rack help solve this problem.

Like poachers, fish boilers use insert racks (colanders work, too) to cover 2-inch-thick steaks or chunks of fatty fish, unpeeled potatoes and peeled onions in water. It takes 20 to 30 minutes of boiling to cook fish. (The resulting rather bland taste can be avoided with some pickling spices or herbs; in Texas, they add chili peppers!)

Steam Cooking

Classic Chinese meals often include a steamed whole fish which is considered a sign of good luck. It's no surprise, then, that one of the best ways to steam fish is in a traditional bamboo steamer. A big pot with just an inch or so of water, wine or flavoring liquid does an excellent job of steaming fish held above the liquid in a colander or rack. Smelt, for example, steam in just three minutes. If you plan to use fish juices as a sauce, you can steam fish on a plate suspended above the liquid.

Steaming's benefits seem manifold. Steam fatty fish and you reduce their calorie content. This is a particularly good method for lake trout. Steam a lean fish and it remains moist and succulent. Add seasonings to the steam-producing liquid and they will be absorbed into the fish.

Steam cooking is great for today's busy world. Dump water into the steamer, place fish on a rack or plate and turn up the heat. If you like, you can stack vegetables in a separate layer above your fish for a one-dish dinner with minimum cleanup. Because water boils at a constant temperature, steam cooking self-regulates; it needs very little attention, and it's faster than boiling.

Pickling

Pickling uses a mix of acidic liquid (usually vinegar, but sometimes citric-acid fluids such as lime or lemon juice) and seasonings to break down fish chemicals and cook it. The result adds a delicious snap to otherwise bland fish, such as smelt. The process was first used by Greek horsemen who would ride on raw meat "saddles" that were tenderized during the day by the rather unlovely combination of the impact between man and beast and their sweat.

A basic pickling mix of 4 cups vinegar, 6 bay leaves, and a tablespoon each of sea salt and pickling spices seems to work best today. After boiling this mixture for 5 minutes, pour the hot pickle solution over smelt and other small fish and refrigerate for about three days. Then enjoy your pickled fish with sour cream or cream cheese on crackers. (When cooked this way, the fish will keep for weeks in the refrigerator.)

Lovely Leftovers

Plan for leftovers and you will save the cook's time. Cooked fish flakes work nicely for fish spreads, fish patties and many other classic dishes. Steaks and chunks can be refrigerated for several days; frozen leftovers store for up to two months.

RECIPES

Bass	Red Mullet
Bluefish	Red Snapper
Bluegill	Salmon
Catfish	Shark
Cod	Snook
Crappie	Sole
Flounder	Striper
Gar	Sturgeon
Halibut	Swordfish
Mackerel	Trout
Mahi Mahi	Tuna
Northern	Walleye
Orange Roughy	Weakfish
Perch	Yellowtail
Redfish	Your Choice

Bass Fillets With Mornay Sauce

Serves: 4
Prep Time: 30 minutes

4 **bass fillets**	¾ **cup Swiss cheese,**
salt and pepper to taste	**grated**
water	¼ **cup sherry**
2 **T. butter**	¼ **cup Parmesan cheese,**
2 **T. flour**	**grated**
1½ **cups milk**	

Place fillets in large skillet and season with salt and pepper. Barely covering fillets with water, simmer until fish flakes easily with fork. Meanwhile, melt butter in saucepan. Add flour and cook until flour browns, stirring constantly. Gradually add cold milk, stirring until well blended. Simmer until thickened. Add Swiss cheese and cook until cheese melts. Add sherry, then remove from heat. Place fish in baking dish and cover with sauce. Sprinkle Parmesan cheese over fish and place in oven under broiler until sauce browns on top. Serve immediately with small, boiled Irish potatoes.

James Fee
St. Paul, Minnesota

Broiled Bass

Serves: 4
Prep Time: 15 minutes

1 **lb. bass fillets**	**lemon juice**
cooking oil	**parsley flakes**
2 **T. melted margarine**	**paprika**

Wash bass fillets and pat dry. Put fish on oiled broiler pan. Brush fish with margarine and drizzle with lemon juice. Add parsley flakes and paprika. Broil until fish is golden brown on one side and flakes easily, about 10-15 minutes.

Nancy German
Pekin, Illinois

Mexican Bass Fillets

Serves: 6
Prep Time: 45 minutes

2 **lbs. bass fillets**
1 **small tomato, chopped**
½ **cup onion, chopped**
½ **cup green pepper,**
   chopped
¼ **cup butter**
¼ **cup green chili salsa**
2 **T. lemon juice**
3 **T. black olives**

1 **T. parsley, minced**
1 **garlic clove, minced**
   salt
   hot pepper sauce
¼ **cup dry white wine**

Combine tomato, onion, green pepper, butter, salsa, lemon juice, olives, parsley, garlic, salt and hot pepper sauce in a 13x9x2-inch baking dish. Bake for about 10 minutes. Stir and add wine. Place fillets on top of sauce and spoon some sauce over fish. Cover and bake for about 20 minutes, depending on thickness of fillets.

Sean Leachman
North Highlands, California

Lemon Pepper Bass

Serves: varies
Prep Time: 3-4 minutes per batch

bass fillets, cut into
bite-sized chunks
1 **egg, beaten**

2 **cups yellow cornmeal**
2 **T. lemon pepper**
   corn oil

Dip bass chunks into beaten egg, then roll in mixture of cornmeal and lemon pepper until covered heavily on each side. Drop battered fish into oil and cook for 3-4 minutes or longer if chunks are larger.

Jim West
Coldwater, Mississippi

Walnut Fried Bass

Serves: 6
Prep Time: 10 minutes

2 lbs. bass fillets	**1 cup flour**
salt and pepper to taste	**2 eggs, beaten**
1½ cups fresh bread crumbs	**⅓ cup butter**
1½ cups walnuts, ground	**⅓ cup oil**
1½ tsp. rosemary, crushed	**lemon wedges**
1 tsp. marjoram leaves	
½ tsp. thyme leaves	

Sprinkle salt and pepper on fillets. Combine bread crumbs, walnuts, rosemary, marjoram and thyme. Roll fillets in flour, then dip in eggs and roll in crumb mixture. Heat butter and oil in frying pan until hot, but not smoking. Place fish in pan and fry at medium heat for 4-5 minutes on each side, or until fish browns and barely flakes when tested with fork. Drain fillets on paper towels. Serve with lemon wedges.

Sean Leachman
North Highlands, California

Baked Bass

Serves: 4
Prep Time: 30 minutes

2 lbs. fish fillets	**lemon pepper**
6 oz. teriyaki sauce	**1 medium onion, thinly sliced**
lemon juice	

Marinate fish overnight in teriyaki sauce. Place fish in bread pan lined with aluminum foil. Sprinkle lemon juice and lemon pepper over fish. Place onion slices on fillets. Cover fillets with foil and bake at 375 degrees for approximately 20-25 minutes.

Eugene Medley
Noble, Louisiana

Terry's Bass Courtbouillon

Serves: 4-6
Prep Time: 2 hours

2 lbs. bass fillets
1 medium onion, chopped
1 bell pepper, chopped
1 garlic clove, finely
  chopped
½ celery stalk, chopped
  butter
4 8-oz. cans tomato sauce
1 can tomatoes with
  jalapeno peppers
1 can cream of mushroom
  soup
  salt
  red pepper
2 cups chicken or fish
  stock

In large, heavy iron pot, brown onion, bell pepper, garlic and celery in butter. Add tomato sauce and tomatoes. Cook on medium flame for 45 minutes. Add cream of mushroom soup, salt and pepper. Stir in stock. Cook another 45 minutes. Add fish fillets and lower heat. Stir occasionally to break up fillets. Cook until tomato sauce has a fairly thick consistency. Serve over white rice.

Terry Abreo
Lutcher, Louisiana

7-Up Bass

Serves: 5
Prep Time: 15 minutes

1 lb. bass fillets
1 cup flour
½ cup cornmeal
1 cup 7-Up soda
  salt and pepper to taste

Cut fillets into small pieces. Combine flour and cornmeal in separate bowl. Dip fillets into 7-Up soda and then in flour-and-cornmeal mixture. Season with salt and pepper and fry until golden brown.

David Knight
Waxahachie, Texas

Stuffed Bass

Serves: 4
Prep Time: 30 minutes

4 fillets, skinned	**1 cup bread crumbs**
2 T. butter	**dash of onion powder**
juice of 1 lemon	**½ tsp. parsley**
¼ tsp. salt	**1 egg, beaten**
¼ tsp. pepper	
1 white bread slice, crumbled	

Lay fillets in shallow baking dish and dot with butter. Drizzle lemon juice over fish. Then season lightly with salt and pepper. Combine white bread, bread crumbs, onion powder, salt, pepper and parsley for stuffing. Add egg and mix. Mound mixture on each fillet. Cover with aluminum foil. Bake in preheated oven at 350 degrees for about 10-15 minutes or until fish flakes.

Joe Terrano
Port Republic, Virginia

Bass Italiano

Serves: 4
Prep Time: 30 minutes

4 fillets, skinned	**1 tsp. onion powder**
1 cup Italian bread crumbs	**½ tsp. salt**
¼ cup cornmeal	**¼ tsp. pepper**
2 T. flour	**1 egg, beaten**
	olive or vegetable oil

Combine dry ingredients. Dip fish in beaten egg and then in crumb mixture. Saute in vegetable or olive oil over medium heat until golden brown.

Joe Terrano
Port Republic, Virginia

White Bass Vegetable Stir-Fry

Serves: 3
Prep Time: 20 minutes

6 white bass fillets
2 tsp. olive oil
1 cup celery, sliced
½ cup onion, chopped

1 pkg. golden bouillon
⅓ cup water
rice (optional)

Put olive oil in frying pan. Add celery and onion and sprinkle with ½ pkg. golden bouillon. Cook over medium-low heat, about 5 minutes, stirring. Add water and cover. Cook until slightly tender. Remove from pan and set aside. Sprinkle remaining ½ pkg. bouillon evenly over fillets (1 side) that have been thoroughly patted dry with paper towels. Place fillets in frying pan, brown lightly on side sprinkled with bouillon. Turn fish. Add vegetables and liquid and cook until fish flakes. Serve with rice, if desired.

Albert Kadet
Painesville, Ohio

Largemouth Delight

Serves: 4
Prep Time: 35 minutes

5½ lbs. bass fillets
3 eggs
¼ cup milk
salt and pepper

sweet basil
lemon peel, grated
flour or cornmeal
butter

In medium-sized bowl, mix eggs, milk, salt and pepper, basil and lemon peel. Place flour on plate. Dip fillets in mixture and submerge. Roll fillets in flour and place in hot skillet with melted butter. Cover and cook on low heat for 10 minutes; turn and cook 5 more minutes.

James Eastridge
North East, Maryland

Southern-Fried Bass

Serves: 2
Prep Time: 1 hour, 30 minutes

1½ lbs. bass fillets
  1 qt. buttermilk
    salt
  1 qt. peanut oil
  1 lb. cornmeal (extra fine)

Cut fillets in strips 1 inch wide. Soak fillets in buttermilk for 1 hour (frozen buttermilk is best). Remove fillets from buttermilk and season with salt to taste. Pour enough oil in frying pan to cover fillets completely. Dredge fillets in cornmeal, then place in heated oil. Using extreme caution, drop a kitchen match into heated oil to determine proper cooking temperature. If match ignites, oil is ready. Do not turn fillets while cooking. When fillets float in heated oil, remove and serve.

Gene Downs
Ozark, Alabama

Broiled Bass Amandine

Serves: 2
Prep Time: 15 minutes

  2 bass fillets (not over 2 lbs.)
  1 lemon, halved
  1 stick butter
  4 T. slivered almonds

Rub cooking pan with half of lemon. In heavy stainless steel pan or iron skillet, melt butter and add juice from half of lemon. Place bass fillets in pan. Squeeze juice from half of lemon over fish. When almost cooked, pour mixture of melted butter and slivered almonds over fish.

A. W. Akira
Knoxville, Tennessee

Cajun Bass And Rice

Serves: 4
Prep Time: 1 hour

1½ **lbs. bass fillets**
 1 **cup mushrooms, sliced**
 ½ **cup red or green pepper, sliced**
 ½ **cup celery, sliced**
 ½ **cup onion, chopped**
 1 **14½-oz. can whole tomatoes (with juice)**
 ¾ **cup chicken broth**
 ¾ **cup long grain rice**
 1 **tsp. paprika**
 ¾ **tsp. dried thyme leaves**
 ¾ **tsp. salt**
 ½ **tsp. dried red pepper**
 ¼ **tsp. ground black pepper**

In 2½- or 3-qt. casserole or baking dish, combine mushrooms, pepper, celery, onion, tomatoes, broth, rice, paprika, thyme, salt and red and black pepper. Cover and bake for 25 minutes at 400 degrees. Stir vegetable-and-rice mixture. Place fish over ingredients in casserole dish. Spoon some sauce over fish. Cover and continue baking for 20 more minutes or until rice is tender and fish flakes easily. Garnish with fresh parsley and lemon if desired. If using microwave: In large microwave-safe baking dish, place all ingredients except fish. Microwave on high power, uncovered, for about 8 minutes. Stir. Place fish fillets on top, cover and vent. Microwave on high power for about 15 minutes more, spooning some juice over fish about every 5 minutes or so.

James Strunk
Philadelphia, Pennsylvania

Cajun Bass Fillets

Serves: 2
Prep Time: 30 minutes

2 large bass fillets
½ T. cajun seasoning
1 medium orange
 tiger sauce
2 tsp. butter or margarine

Sprinkle cajun seasoning on fillets. Cut 2 orange slices from orange. Squeeze juice from remaining orange on each fillet. Add 3 drops tiger sauce to each fillet and place on hot grill. Melt butter or margarine and drop on fillets while cooking. (Do not flip fillets.) Cook for approximately 20 minutes or until fillets are flaky. Garnish with orange slices.

Stephen Larimore
Louisville, Kentucky

Sea Bass Amandine

Serves: 4
Prep Time: 20 minutes

2 lbs. sea bass fillets
 fresh lemon juice
 flour
6 T. butter
1 cup slivered blanched
 almonds
 salt and pepper
 parsley, chopped

Dip fillets in lemon juice, then in flour. Saute fish in butter until delicately browned on both sides. Remove fillets to heated platter. Brown almonds very quickly. Season fillets with salt and pepper to taste. Drizzle with lemon juice and sprinkle with parsley. Pour almond mixture over hot fillets and serve at once.

T. Eisenhauer
Rockaway, New York

Cajun Bass

Serves: 4
Prep Time: 10 minutes

2 lbs. bass fillets
¼ cup melted butter
salt and pepper to taste
½ tsp. cajun spice
¼ tsp. onion salt
¼ tsp. paprika
¼ tsp. garlic salt

Preheat barbecue grill or prepare open fire. Lay fillets flat on aluminum foil. (Do not overlap.) Baste fillets with butter. Sprinkle remaining ingredients evenly over fillets. Wrap heavy-duty aluminum foil around fillets, making a sealed cooking bag. Make sure to seal tightly so no steam escapes. Place bag on grill and cook for 7-10 minutes. (Do not flip.) Use caution when opening foil.

Darren Ratliff
Tauares, Florida

Fried Bass Fingers

Serves: 4
Prep Time: 20 minutes

4 bass fillets
dry pancake mix
ginger ale
cooking oil

Cut bass fillets into finger-sized strips. Mix thick batter from pancake mix and ginger ale. Heat oil in frying pan. Dip bass strips into batter and drop into oil to deep-fry. Remove bass strips when done. Drain excess oil on paper towels. Serve strips with tartar sauce or shrimp cocktail sauce.

Kevin Arrant
Sarasota, Florida

Tart & Tangy Bass

Serves: 4
Prep Time: 15 minutes

2 lbs. bass fillets	**1 tsp. tarragon**
cooking oil	**lime wedges**
¼ cup margarine	**parsley sprigs**
1 T. lemon juice	
lemon pepper	
¼ tsp. orange peel, grated	
½ tsp. salt	

Put oil in pan and preheat broiler. Place fillets in pan and baste with mixture made of melted margarine, lemon juice, lemon pepper, orange peel, salt and tarragon. Broil for 10 minutes or until flaky while brushing fillets often with above mixture. Serve with lime wedges and parsley sprigs.

Ronald Musgrave
Darby, Montana

Bass 'N' Peppers

Serves: 5
Prep Time: 20 minutes

1 lb. bass fillets	**2 medium green peppers**
3 T. soy sauce	**(cut into 1-inch pieces)**
1 garlic clove, chopped	**8 oz. mushrooms, halved**
¼ tsp. ground ginger	**3 T. vegetable oil**

Mix soy sauce, garlic and ginger. Brush mixture on both sides of fish. In 10-inch skillet, cook green peppers and mushrooms in oil over medium heat until crispy, about 6 minutes. Then fry fish separately from vegetables until they flake easily, about 8-10 minutes. Add vegetables and heat until all is hot. Serve with rice.

Mike Sheppard
Escatawapa, Mississippi

Bass With Dijon & Peppercorn Sauce

Serves: 4
Prep Time: 30 minutes

- **1 lb. fresh bass**
  salt and pepper to taste
- **4 oz. butter**
- **2 oz. white wine**
- **½ oz. peppercorns**
- **2 cups heavy whipping**
  cream
- **2 oz. Dijon mustard**

Clean, skin and bone bass. Place fish in baking pan in 4-oz. portions. Season with salt and pepper. Add 4 oz. melted butter, salt and 1 oz. white wine. Cover with aluminum foil and bake at 350 degrees until consistently cooked, about 15-20 minutes. Heat saucepan. Add peppercorns, 1 oz. wine, heavy whipping cream and Dijon mustard. Cook until you have a sauce.

Buddy Allphin
New Richmond, Ohio

Steamed Bass

Serves: 4
Prep Time: 30 minutes

- **2 large bass**
- **4-5 celery stalks, chopped**
  water
- **¼ cup margarine, melted**
- **½-1 T. lemon pepper**

Place chopped celery in glass baking dish. Add enough water to cover celery. Lay fish on top and brush with butter. Sprinkle lemon pepper over fish. Cover and bake at 375 degrees for approximately 20 minutes or until fish is light and flaky. Serve over rice or pasta.

Mike Bigall
Redding, California

Smoked Bass Fillet

Serves: 4
Prep Time: 30 minutes

- **1 lb. bass fillets**
- **½ cup liquid smoke**
- **¼ cup prime rib rub**
- **2 T. butter or margarine**

Preheat oven to 350 degrees. Pour liquid smoke into shallow dish. Dip fillets in liquid smoke, soaking both sides. Place fillets in shallow baking pan, making sure fillets are not touching. Sprinkle prime rib rub on fillets and place in oven. After allowing it to bake 5-7 minutes, lightly brush melted butter on each fillet. Bake until they flake easily, about 10-15 minutes.

James Hodgdon
Kansas City, Missouri

Pimiento Glazed Bass

Serves: 4
Prep Time: 10 minutes

- **1½ lbs. bass fillets**
- **½-1 tsp. salt**
- **2 T. lemon juice**
- **½ tsp. dried thyme leaves**
- **¼ tsp. Dijon mustard**
- **½ cup sour cream**
- **2 T. pimiento, chopped**
- **1 T. green onion, minced**

Season fillets with salt, lemon juice and thyme. Place fillets in lightly buttered baking dish. Cover tightly. Bake at 400 degrees for 8-10 minutes. Uncover and glaze with a mixture of mustard, sour cream, pimiento and green onion. Return to oven and bake 2-3 minutes longer. Serve on warm platter.

Michael Berge
North Bend, Oregon

Southern-Grilled Bass

Serves: 2
Prep Time: 30 minutes

1½ lbs. bass fillets
1 qt. mayonnaise or salad
   dressing
6 oz. soy sauce

Fillet bass leaving skin and scales on one side, but bone completely. Mix mayonnaise and soy sauce until color of mixture matches a new copper penny. Cover entire surface of each fillet side with mixture. Place on charcoal grill, skin-side toward heated coals. Do not turn. When edges turn up and scales flake, remove and serve.

Gene Downs
Ozark, Alabama

TJ's Blackened Bass

Serves: 4
Prep Time: 1 hour

8 8-oz. bass fillets
   blackening seasoning
1 stick butter

Season fillets with blackening seasoning. Melt butter and pour over seasoned fillets. Place heavy, cast-iron skillet on heat source allowing skillet to become white hot. Place 2 fillets at a time in skillet. (Expect to see plenty of smoke.) When fillets get white near the middle, approximately 45-60 seconds, flip them over. After removing fillets from skillet, wait until skillet gets hot again before adding more fillets. Serve with baked potato.

Terry Abreo
Lutcher, Louisiana

Larry's Bluefish Bake

Serves: varies
Prep Time: 30 minutes

bluefish fillets	**salt**
bread slices	**pepper**
mayonnaise	**parsley**
flavored bread crumbs	

Rinse fresh fillets and pat dry. In shallow baking pan, place bread slices to cover bottom. Place fillets on bread (with fish's dark-side down). Generously spread mayonnaise over fillets. Season to taste with bread crumbs, salt, pepper and parsley. Bake at 350 degrees until fish flakes, approximately 15 minutes. When serving, remove fillets from bread.

Larry Irish
Niantic, Connecticut

Broiled Bay Bluefish

Serves: 3
Prep Time: 1 hour

3 lbs. bluefish	**½ cup onion, chopped**
3 T. butter or margarine	**¼ cup lemon juice**
½ cup green pepper,	**3 tsp. black pepper**
chopped	**salt**

Clean and remove head and tail of bluefish and place in baking pan. Rub butter over and inside fish. Sprinkle pepper and onion over and inside fish. Pour lemon juice over and inside fish, adding salt to taste. Sprinkle with additional pepper, if desired. Broil fish for 20 minutes, checking every 5 minutes until slightly brown on edges. Serve with Italian bread and salad if desired.

Scott Schrauth
Ridgewood, New York

Bluegill With Zucchini

Serves: 4
Prep Time: 20 minutes

12 bluegills, pan-fried
3-4 zucchini, 4-6 inches
　　long
　1 can pimiento, drained
　　and cut into strips
　1 T. cider vinegar

After frying fish, put in warm covered bowl. Drain all but a light film of oil from the skillet. Trim ends and wash zucchini. Slice at a very sharp angle, almost lengthwise, into slices ¼-½ inch thick. Saute zucchini in remaining oil in skillet. Cook about 1 minute per slice over medium-high heat. Add pimiento strips and fish; stir. Cover pan, retaining heat to keep fish warm. Remove and serve. (Lemon juice can be used in place of vinegar if you prefer.)

Jeffery Shaver
Wayland, New York

Panfish Marinade

Serves: varies
Prep Time: 10 minutes

　　bluegill fillets
　2 cups milk
　¼ cup mustard
　2½ T. liquid crab boil
　4 T. creole seasoning
　½ cup mayonnaise

Mix ingredients (except fish) in large bowl and stir thoroughly. Add panfish and marinate for approximately 1 hour. Bread fillets, fry and serve.

David Pelliching
Hammond, Louisiana

Fried Bluegills

Serves: 4
Prep Time: 25-30 minutes

> **bluegill fillets**
> 1 **cup cornflake crumbs**
> ½ **cup flour**
> ¼ **cup yellow cornmeal**
> 1 **large egg**
> 1 **tsp. milk**
> **cooking oil**

Mix cornflake crumbs, flour and cornmeal together and put in plastic bag. Combine egg and milk. Dip fish in egg and milk mixture. Shake fillets in plastic bag with coating mixture. To pan-fry, use 2 tsp. cooking oil and cook slow. To fry in deep-fryer, heat oil to 360 degrees and fry fillets for about 2-3 minutes.

Richard Scott
Conneaut, Ohio

Bluegill Salad

Serves: 4
Prep Time: 15 minutes

> **4 bluegill fillets**
> **4 eggs, hard-cooked**
> **1 large celery stalk**
> **1 small onion, grated**
> **1 can tiny peas**

> **1½ T. sweet pickle or relish**
> **mayonnaise or salad dressing**
> **salt and pepper to taste**

Boil fillets until meat falls apart, about 5 minutes. Mix all ingredients together, adding enough salad dressing to moisten. Season with salt and pepper to taste.

John Linstman
Fulton, Indiana

Baked Bluegills

Serves: 4
Prep Time: 25-30 minutes

6-8 bluegill fillets
  1 cup onion, chopped
  3 T. margarine
2½ T. flour
  ½ cup catsup
  **1 can condensed
    consomme**
  **¾ cup dill pickles, thinly
    sliced**

Saute onions in margarine. Gradually stir in flour, adding catsup and consomme. Simmer for 20 minutes, stirring occasionally. Add sliced pickles and place fish in baking dish. Cover with sauce. Bake at 400 degrees for 25-30 minutes or until fish flakes.

Kenneth Schell
Mandan, North Dakota

Quick And Easy
Beer Battered Bluegills

Serves: varies
Prep Time: 20 minutes

  1 lb. bluegill fillets
  2 cups dry pancake batter
  **1 can beer
    salt and pepper to taste
    dash of garlic powder**

Rinse fillets and dip in dry pancake batter. Then mix 2 cups pancake batter, using beer in place of water. For a thicker coating, use less beer. Add remaining ingredients to pancake mix. Dip fillets in batter and fry in hot oil until golden brown.

Leo Wiskirski
Summit Hill, Pennsylvania

Crispy Fried Catfish

Serves: 6
Prep Time: 2 hours, 30 minutes

- **6 medium catfish, cleaned and dressed**
- **1 tsp. salt**
- **¼ tsp. pepper**
- **1 2-oz. bottle hot sauce**
- **2 cups self-rising cornmeal**
  vegetable oil
  watercress (optional)
  lemon slices (optional)

Sprinkle salt and pepper over catfish. Place catfish in shallow dish and add hot sauce. Marinate for 1-2 hours in refrigerator. Place cornmeal in plastic bag. Drop catfish in bag one at a time and shake until completely coated. Fry fish in deep, hot oil (375 degrees) until fish float to the top and are golden brown. Drain well. Garnish with watercress and lemon slices if desired.

Charles Fish
Smithville, Tennessee

Marinated Catfish

Serves: 4
Prep Time: 15 minutes

- **1 lb. catfish fillets**
- **½ cup soy sauce**
- **2 T. lemon juice**
- **1 T. Worcestershire sauce**
- **2 garlic cloves**

Mix all ingredients. Marinate fish in mixture overnight. Cook on grill or in electric skillet.

Linda Hixson
Barling, Arkansas

Catfish Stew

Serves: 8
Prep Time: 40 minutes

**4 medium catfish, cleaned
    and dressed**
4 cups water
**4 cups potatoes, peeled
    and dried**
2 cups onions, chopped
**2 cups corn kernels,
    drained**

1 T. butter
salt and pepper to taste
2 cups milk

Simmer catfish in water until fish flakes from bone. Remove fish and strain, reserving liquid. Remove and discard fish bones. Set meat aside. Add potatoes, onions and corn to reserved liquid. Simmer mixture on low heat for 20 minutes or until vegetables are tender. Stir in butter, salt and pepper, milk and reserved fish meat. Heat thoroughly.

Susan Cook
Holcomb, New York

Sesame Parmesan Catfish

Serves: 6
Prep Time: 30 minutes

**6 catfish fillets, cut into
    1-inch squares**
1 cup flour
1 egg, beaten
½ cup sesame seeds
½ cup Parmesan cheese

Roll fillets in flour. Then dip fish in egg and roll in mixture of sesame seeds and Parmesan cheese. Deep-fry.

Linda Hixson
Barling, Arkansas

Cajun Catfish

Serves: 4
Prep Time: 30 minutes

**6 small catfish, cleaned
  and dressed**
1 tsp. salt (optional)
¼ tsp. fresh black pepper
1 2-oz. bottle hot sauce

salt and pepper to taste
**2 cups cornmeal,
  self-rising**
olive oil

Combine salt, pepper and hot sauce to create marinade.
Season catfish with salt and pepper to taste and marinate for
1-2 hours in refrigerator. Put cornmeal into paper bag. Drop
catfish in bag, one at a time, and shake bag until fish are
completely coated. Fry fish in deep, hot olive oil (375 degrees)
until fish float to surface and are golden brown. Drain on paper
towels and serve hot.

Susan Cook
Holcomb, New York

Southern Catfish Stew

Serves: 15
Prep Time: 1 hour, 30 minutes

3 medium-sized catfish
½ lb. salt pork, cubed
1 lb. onion, cubed
2 lbs. white potatoes

1 6-oz. can tomato paste
½ cup butter or margarine
salt and pepper to taste

Simmer fish in 6-qt. pan with enough water to cover fish. Cook
for 30-45 minutes. Remove fish from broth and bone. Fry pork
until brown. Place fish, pork, onions and potatoes in broth.
Cook until tender. Add remaining ingredients and simmer for
30 minutes.

Gynita Sumter
Elgin, South Carolina

Catfish Veracruz

Serves: 4
Prep Time: 45 minutes

- 1 **lb. catfish fillets**
- 1 **medium onion, thinly sliced**
- 1 **garlic clove, minced**
- 2 **T. olive oil**
- 1 **16-oz. can stewed tomatoes**
- 1 **bay leaf**
- ¼ **tsp. oregano leaves**
- ½ **tsp. salt**
- ¼ **tsp. pepper**
- 1 **T. capers**
- 1 **T. lemon juice**
- 2 **T. green chilies**

In skillet, saute onion and garlic until clear. Add tomatoes, herbs, salt and pepper and simmer for 10 minutes uncovered. Add remaining ingredients, including catfish. Cover and simmer gently for 7½ minutes on each side.

Chuck Pemberton
Phoenix, Arizona

Spicy Hot Catfish (Grilled)

Serves: 4-6
Prep Time: 1 hour

4 **lbs. catfish fillets**	1 **large sweet onion**
2 **cups milk**	4 **hot banana peppers**
Old Bay seafood	4 **hot chili peppers**
seasoning	**salt**

Rinse and dry fillets. Soak in milk for 30 minutes. Remove from milk and rinse, removing excess moisture. Sprinkle with seasoning, rubbing it into meat. Start grill and place ⅛-inch-thick onion slices on grill. Slice banana peppers and place on top of onion slices. Place fish on top of onion and pepper. Thinly slice chili peppers and sprinkle over fish. Cover loosely with aluminum foil. Grill until easily flaked. Salt to taste.

Roy Woods
Big Rapids, Michigan

Fried Catfish

Serves: 4-6
Prep Time: 15 minutes

2 **lbs. catfish**	2 **tsp. milk**
2 **tsp. salt**	1½ **cups cornmeal**
¼ **tsp. pepper**	**vegetable oil or**
2 **eggs, beaten**	**shortening**

Season fish with salt and pepper. Combine eggs and milk. Dip fish into egg mixture, then roll in cornmeal to coat. Pour oil into frying pan, filling to the half-way point; heat to 370 degrees. Fry fillets for 7-8 minutes or until first side is golden brown, then turn and cook 7-8 more minutes until fish flakes easily with fork. Drain fillets on paper towels and serve.

Nate Gadzik
Mesa, Arizona

Broiled Mexican Catfish Fillets

Serves: 4-6
Prep Time: 15 minutes

2-3 lbs. catfish fillets
1½ cups melted butter
½ cup lemon juice
dill weed
2 16-oz. jars salsa (mild or hot)
3-4 cups rice (cooked)

Cut catfish fillets in 6-8 chunks per fillet. Put in baking dish large enough to lay fish flat. Melt butter, add lemon juice and heat. Pour mixture over fish and lightly sprinkle with dill weed. Broil about 8-10 minutes or until fish is flaky. Remove from oven, pour salsa over fish and heat an additional 5 minutes. Serve fish over rice with Mexican corn bread.

Bill Henley Jr.
Hopewell, Virginia

Crispy Catfish

Serves: 4
Prep Time: 30 minutes

2 pan-dressed catfish
⅓ cup cornmeal
⅓ cup flour
1 tsp. salt
½ tsp. paprika
¼ tsp. onion powder

⅛ tsp. pepper
1 egg beaten
1 T. water
½ cup shortening

Combine cornmeal, flour, salt, paprika, onion powder and pepper on waxed paper. Combine eggs and water in shallow dish or pie plate. Dip fish in egg mixture, then coat with cornmeal mixture. Heat oil in electric skillet at 365 degrees or on medium-high heat in large, heavy skillet. Fry fish for 10 minutes on each side or until crispy or brown.

Bill Daniel
Marshall, Arkansas

Spicy Catfish

Serves: 4
Prep Time: 30 minutes

2 pan-dressed catfish	**½ tsp. paprika**
hot sauce	**¼ tsp. onion powder**
⅓ cup cornmeal	**⅛ tsp. pepper**
⅓ cup flour	**½ cup shortening**
1 tsp. salt	

In refrigerator, marinate catfish overnight in hot sauce. Cut fish in half lengthwise. Combine cornmeal, flour, salt, paprika, onion powder and pepper on waxed paper. Roll fish in mix. Heat shortening in electric skillet at 365 degrees or on medium-high heat in large, heavy skillet. Fry fish for 10 minutes on each side.

Bill Daniel
Marshall, Arkansas

LaSoy Catfish

Serves: 4
Prep Time: 3 hours

2 lbs. catfish fillets	**1 egg**
½ cup soy sauce	**1 cup milk**
1 tsp. garlic powder	**seasoned bread crumbs**
(heaping)	**2 cups vegetable oil**
1 tsp. black pepper	**1 cup olive oil**

Place fillets in bowl or container. Add soy sauce, garlic powder and black pepper and marinate for 2 hours or longer. Pat dry on paper towels. Mix egg and milk together in separate bowl. Dip marinated fillets in egg mixture and then in crumbs. Heat oils together in frying pan and fry fillets for approximately 1½ minutes on each side or until brown.

Michael Lozak
Parlin, New Jersey

Salt Cod And Peanut Stew

Serves: 6-8
Prep Time: 24 hours

2 lbs. hard salt cod	1 lb. green frying pepper
¼ cup olive oil	1 1-lb. yellow summer
1 3-oz. yellow onion	squash, chunked
2 tsp. curry powder	½ lb. shelled unroasted
12 white onions	peanuts
12 small white onions	4 tsp. grated lemon rind
1½ lbs. fresh plum tomatoes	2 cups cooked rice

Soak cod for 24 hours, changing water three times. Drain cod
and transfer to deep skillet. Cover cod with cold water. Bring
to a boil and simmer for 10 minutes. Strain and save liquid.
Turn cod pieces out onto cloth towel and cut into chunks.
Remove skin and bones. Heat oil. Saute minced yellow onion
and add curry powder. Cook, stirring until brown. Peel onions
and tomatoes. Stir in whole white onions, squared peppers,
squash and 5 cups poaching liquid. Bring to boil. Reduce to
simmer and add peanuts and lemon rind. Simmer for 1 hour or
until peanuts are tender. When peanuts are done, add cod.
Simmer for 5 minutes. Serve over rice.

Paul Grimes
Rio Rancho, New Mexico

Poached Cod

Serves: 4
Prep Time: 20 minutes

4 cod fillets	1 tsp. salt
2-3 cups water	1 tsp. fresh parsley
2-3 bay leaves	½ medium onion, diced

Cut fish into serving-sized pieces. Put all ingredients, except
fish, into skillet. Simmer for 5 minutes. Add fish and simmer
again for 5 minutes.

Eric Eckenrode
Dover, Pennsylvania

Pam's Head Chowder

Serves: 2
Prep Time: 30 minutes

cod head	**3-4 medium potatoes,**
cold water	**peeled and diced**
1 small piece salt pork,	**2 cups cream**
diced	**2-4 T. butter**
2 onions, thinly sliced	**salt and pepper to taste**

Rinse cod head and place in pot of cold water. Cook until tender at slow boil. Strain fish from broth, returning broth to stove and reserving fish head. Fry salt pork until nicely browned. Remove pork piece. Add 2 T. pork grease to fish stock. In remaining grease, fry onions until golden and add to stock. Then add potatoes and cook until tender. Add fish, cream and pork and simmer slowly for 3-5 minutes. Add butter, salt and pepper. Serve with fresh hot bread.

Larry Irish
Niantic, Connecticut

Poached Lemon Fish

Serves: 4
Prep Time: 20 minutes

2 lbs. cod	**1 garlic clove, crushed**
1 fresh lemon	**salt**
6-8 whole peppercorns	**½ stick butter, melted**

In large skillet half filled with water, slice lemon. Add peppercorns, garlic and salt. Boil for 10 minutes. Reduce heat and gently add fish. (Do not overlay.) Simmer for 5 minutes. Carefully turn fish. Simmer for 10-15 minutes until done. Serve with lemon and drizzle with melted butter.

J. Malinowski
Royal Oak, Michigan

Parmesan Baked Cod

Serves: 4-6
Prep Time: 30 minutes

3 lbs. cod fillets
1 cup bread crumbs or
crushed cornflakes
½ cup Parmesan cheese,
grated

1 tsp. dry thyme leaves
1½ tsp. paprika
½ cup melted butter or
margarine

Rinse and pat dry fish. Cut fillets into square pieces. Combine bread crumbs, cheese, thyme leaves and paprika in bowl. Put butter in separate, shallow bowl. Dip fish in butter, then into dry cheese and crumb mixture to thickly coat. Place fillets 1 inch apart into shallow-rimmed baking pan lined with aluminum foil. Bake uncovered at 425 degrees for 10-12 minutes.

Todd Streit
Pasadena, California

Bailey's Fish And Chips

Serves: varies
Prep Time: 30-45 minutes

cod fish fillets
whole milk
4 eggs
flour

potatoes
water
salt
oil

Soak fillets in whole milk for 1 hour. Pat dry with paper towel. Combine eggs and 1 cup milk. Dip fish in egg mixture, then dredge in flour. Fry until fillets are golden and crisp. Cut up potatoes with skins on and soak in salted water for 30 minutes. Pat dry. Fry in 300-degree oil for 1 minute. Remove and cool at room temperature. Put back in 365-degree oil until done.

Michael Bailey
Nineveh, Indiana

Crappie Delight

Serves: 4-6
Prep Time: 1 hour

4 lbs. crappie fillets	**¼ tsp. seasoning salt**
½ cup creamy Italian dressing	**¼ tsp. pepper**
2 green onions, finely chopped	**1 cup mozzarella cheese, grated**
	1 lemon, wedged

Marinate fillets in dressing for 30 minutes. Remove and place evenly in baking dish. Pour remaining dressing over fillets. Sprinkle onions, seasoning salt and pepper over fish. Bake at 350 degrees for approximately 12 minutes. Pull dish from oven and sprinkle cheese over fillets. Return dish to oven and bake 8 more minutes. Remove and let cool, about 2 minutes. Put fillets on plates, cheese-side down. Squeeze lemon wedges over fish and serve.

Kevin Kekic
Tucson, Arizona

Cajun-Style Crappies

Serves: 4
Prep Time: 1 hour

8 crappie fillets
½ cup flour
dash of salt
dash of pepper
cajun seasoning to taste
½ cup milk
½ cup oil

Mix flour, salt, pepper and cajun seasoning together. Dip fillets in milk, then in flour mixture. Make sure to coat fillets completely. Fry fillets in oil until golden brown.

Daniel Wood
Pringle, South Dakota

Healthy And Quick Crappies

Serves: 2
Prep Time: 10 minutes

½-¾ lb. fish fillets
2-3 T. margarine, melted
salt and pepper
your favorite seasonings

Place fillets in shallow, microwave baking dish. (Do not overlap fillets.) Cover by rubbing melted margarine over fillets. Season with salt and pepper to taste. Top with your favorite seasonings (cajun seasoning or garlic and paprika). Cook in microwave on high for 4 minutes. Serve with white or brown rice and a salad.

Shirley Wilburn
San Antonio, Texas

Red-Headed Spicy Crappie Grill Bake

Serves: 4
Prep Time: 15 minutes

1 lb. crappie fillets
½ lb. fresh mushrooms, sliced
½ stick margarine, softened
¼ tsp. garlic powder
½ cup medium picante sauce

Combine all ingredients in pie tin lined with aluminum foil. Seal foil and place on prepared grill. Cook for 15-20 minutes, or bake in oven for 20-25 minutes at 325 degrees. Serve over steaming hot rice.

Glenn Strayer
Algona, Iowa

Buttermilk Crappies

Serves: 6
Prep Time: 45 minutes

- **2 lbs. crappie fillets**
- **12 oz. buttermilk**
- **6 oz. beer or 7-Up**
- **1 tsp. Kitchen Klatter**
- **1 tsp. soy sauce**
- **1 lb. cornmeal**
- **2 cups flour**
- **3 T. lemon pepper**
- **3 T. seasoned black pepper**
- **3 T. seasoned salt**
  salt to taste
  peanut oil

Combine buttermilk, beer, Kitchen Klatter and soy sauce in large bowl. Mix together well and set aside. In large bag, combine cornmeal, flour, lemon pepper, seasoned pepper, seasoned salt and table salt. Shake well to mix ingredients. Dip crappie fillets in buttermilk mixture and then in bag. Shake well to coat fillets. Deep-fry in peanut oil until golden brown.

John Stark
Eldon, Missouri

Lawrey's-Adkins' Crappie

Serves: 3 fillets per person
Prep Time: 30 minutes

fillets
Lawrey's seasoned salt
Adkins dry rub
bold and spicy mustard
flour
cornmeal
peanut oil

Sprinkle fillets with seasoned salt and Adkins rub. Let fillets stand for about 15-20 minutes. Dip fillets in equal parts of hot mustard and water. Roll in equal parts of flour and cornmeal. Deep fry in peanut oil at 350 degrees for 3-5 minutes.

Mike Glover
Dallas, Texas

Crunchy Oven-Fried Crappie

Serves: 4
Prep Time: 20 minutes

3 lbs. crappie fillets
⅓ cup nonfat yogurt
½ cup Dijon mustard
1 T. lemon juice
¾ cup corn chips, finely crushed
½ tsp. thyme

Heat oven to 450 degrees. Mix yogurt, mustard and lemon juice. Dip fish into mixture, coat with chips and place in buttered baking dish. Bake uncovered for 10-12 minutes, or until fish flakes easily with fork.

LeeRoy Wilson
Omaha, Nebraska

Cucumber Crappies

Serves: 4
Prep Time: 20 minutes

1½ **lbs. crappie fillets**
   butter
 ½ **cup cucumber, chopped**
 1 **cup salad dressing or**
   mayonnaise
 1 **tsp. dried dill weed**
 2 **green onions, chopped**
 ½ **tsp. lemon juice**
 4 **drops Tabasco sauce**

Butter large oven-proof platter. Lay fillets on platter and cover with ingredients. Broil 4 inches from heat in preheated oven until top is brown, about 5-10 minutes. Serve over rice.

Conrad Eck
Ellenville, New York

Italian Fried Fish

Serves: 6
Prep Time: 1 hour, 10 minutes

 4 **lbs. crappie fillets**
10-12 **oz. Italian dressing**
 2 **cups crackers, crushed**
 1 **cup Parmesan cheese,**
   grated
   peanut oil

Marinate fillets in salad dressing for at least 1 hour. Mix crackers and cheese. Shake fillets in mixture and deep-fry at 400 degrees for 3-5 minutes or until golden brown.

Mike Stover
Dallas, Texas

Prawn Rolled Flounder

Serves: 2-3
Prep Time: 1 hour

12 flounder, filleted	**2 oz. blue cheese**
12 medium prawns, cleaned, chopped and cooked	**1½ T. onion, minced**
	1½ tsp. parsley, minced
½ cup butter	**10 drops Tabasco sauce**
2 oz. cream cheese	**dash of pepper**
	1 T. lemon juice

Combine all ingredients (except fish). Chill mixture for at least 15 minutes. Spread mixture over fillets and roll. Pin with toothpicks. Put fish in buttered casserole dish. Ladle melted butter over each roll and bake for 15-20 minutes at 375 degrees.

William Banducci
Concord, California

Bar-B-Qued Door Mat

Serves: 2
Prep Time: 10 minutes

1 whole flounder
5 bacon strips, cooked and chopped
2 green onions or chives, chopped
3 T. butter
1 celery stalk, chopped
½ lemon, sliced

Place flounder in aluminum foil. Add bacon, green onion, butter, celery and lemon to fish. Wrap tightly. Drop foil onto coals for about 2 minutes, then flip for another 2 minutes. Open foil and let fish simmer on grill until cooked as desired.

Mario Moline Jr.
Brownsville, Texas

Flounder Provencale

Serves: 6
Prep Time: 45 minutes

- **6 flounder fillets**
- **4 T. butter**
  salt
  paprika
- **¼ cup onion, chopped**
- **1 garlic clove, minced**
- **1 1-lb. can tomatoes, chopped**
- **1 3-oz. can mushrooms, drained and chopped**
- **¼ cup dry white wine**
- **6 lemon wedges**
  parsley sprigs

Put 2 tsp. butter on each fillet. Season with salt and paprika, then roll up fillets. Fasten fillets with toothpicks. Place rolled fillets in skillet. Add onion, garlic, tomatoes, mushrooms and wine. Cover tightly and simmer for about 15 minutes or until fish flakes easily. Remove fish to warm platter. Simmer sauce until slightly thickened. Spoon sauce over fish rolls. Garnish with lemon wedges and parsley sprigs.

Scott Chastain
Haines City, Florida

Gar Balls

Serves: 6-12
Prep Time: 10 minutes

2 lbs. gar meat, flaked
½ cup prepared yellow
   mustard
½ cup vinegar
1 lb. potatoes, mashed
2 large onions, finely
   chopped

1 cup parsley
1 cup green onions
1 cup celery tops
flour
cooking oil

Make sauce by mixing mustard and vinegar. Mix meat, potatoes, onions and vegetables. Shape this mixture into balls with ½-inch diameters. Roll balls in mustard sauce and flour and deep-fry in cooking oil.

Art Harris
Jupiter, Florida

Garfish Balls

Serves: 5-10
Prep Time: 1 hour

5 lbs. garfish
2½ lbs. tator tots or frozen
   precooked potatoes
1 onion, chopped
1 garlic clove, minced
1 bell pepper, chopped
   creole seasoning

Cut fish into small pieces. Boil until fish is white throughout. In equal parts, mix fish, potatoes, onion, garlic, bell pepper and seasoning in coarse meat grinder. Form mixture into small balls (a little larger than golf balls). Deep-fry until dark brown.

Paul Pontiff
Baldwin, Louisiana

Foil-Baked Fish

Serves: 2
Prep Time: 30-35 minutes

2 **4-oz. halibut fillets**	1 **carrot**
1 **shallot, minced**	1 **small zucchini**
2 **tsp. olive oil**	4 **mushroom caps**
2 **green onions**	4 **canned water chestnuts**
1 **leek (white part only)**	1 **T. lime or lemon juice**
1 **tsp. fresh ginger root,**	2 **tsp. soy sauce**
peeled and grated	**fresh white pepper**

Saute shallot in oil for 30 seconds. Add thinly sliced green
onions, leek and ginger root. Cook for 1 minute. Thinly slice
carrot, zucchini, mushrooms and water chestnuts; add to
mixture, stirring over heat for about 2 minutes. Add juice, soy
sauce and pepper. Place fillets on aluminum foil and top with
vegetables. Fold foil over and crimp edges. Bake for 8-10
minutes per inch of thickness of fish at 450 degrees.

Richard Filsinger
Honolulu, Hawaii

Rosemary's Halibut

Serves: 4-6
Prep Time: 15-20 minutes

2 **lbs. halibut steaks**	2 **T. water**
flour	3 **garlic cloves, peeled**
salt and pepper to taste	**and washed**
1/3 **cup olive oil**	1/2 **tsp. rosemary**
1/4 **cup white wine vinegar**	

Cut fish into 3x5-inch pieces and coat with flour. Season with
salt and pepper. Heat oil to medium-hot. Cook fish for 5
minutes per side. Remove and keep warm. Combine vinegar,
water, garlic and rosemary. Boil until volume is reduced by
half. Remove garlic. Spoon over fish. Serve over hot rice.

Richard Seymour
Julian, California

A Parcel For The Halibut

Serves: 6
Prep Time: 20-30 minutes

1 **lb. halibut fillets, cut in sixths**
  kitchen parchment paper
1 **tsp. dried oregano**
½ **tsp. garlic powder**
1 **cup shallots, chopped**
1 **cup tomatoes, peeled and chopped**
2 **oz. feta cheese, crumbled**
  fresh ground pepper
2 **T. chopped cilantro**
1 **lemon, sliced**

Preheat oven to 400 degrees. Cut parchment paper in 12- to 14-inch squares. Fold in half and trim in heart shape. Place halibut portion close to parchment's center crease. Sprinkle oregano and garlic powder over fillets. Divide shallots and tomatoes equally over fish. Follow with feta cheese. Season to taste with ground pepper and cilantro. Top with lemon slices. Fold over remaining side of parchment paper. Starting with round edges, pleat and crimp edges together to make a seal, twisting ends slightly. Spray top of parchment with non-sticking spray. Place side by side on baking sheet. Bake 12 minutes or until parchment is browned. Cut parcels open and serve. Garnish with fresh parsley and lemon wedges.

Lee Gardner
Corvallis, Oregon

Fish Kabobs

Serves: 6
Prep Time: 30 minutes

1½ lbs. halibut steaks	**1 garlic clove, minced**
¼ cup lime juice	**3 small zucchini and/or**
2 T. olive oil	**yellow squash, sliced**
1 T. parsley flakes	**1 red sweet pepper, sliced**
1 tsp. ground cumin	**½ lb. small pearl onions**

Cut fish into 1-inch cubes. Add next 5 ingredients into ¼ cup
water. Pour over fish. Marinate for 38 minutes turning twice.
Precook vegetables for 2-3 minutes in boiling water. Drain
vegetables and fish, reserving marinade. Thread fish and
vegetable onto 6 skewers; brush with marinade. Place kabobs
on broiler rack, and broil 3-4 inches from heat source for 3-5
minutes on each side. Brush with marinade. Serve with rice.

Lee Gardner
Corvallis, Oregon

Halibut Kabobs

Serves: 6
Prep Time: 30 minutes

1½ lbs. halibut steaks	**¼ cup water**
¼ cup lime juice	**3 small zucchini and/or**
2 T. olive oil	**yellow squash, cut in**
1 T. parsley flakes	**¾-inch slices**
1 tsp. ground cumin	**1 red pepper, chopped**
1 garlic clove, minced	**½ lb. small pearl onions**

Cut fish into 1-inch cubes. Combine lime juice, olive oil, parsley
flakes, cumin, garlic and water. Pour mixture over fish and
marinate for 30 minutes, turning twice. Precook vegetables for
2-3 minutes in boiling water. Drain vegetables and fish; reserve
marinade. Thread fish and vegetables onto 6 skewers. Brush
with marinade and broil until done. Serve with rice if desired.

Lee Gardner
Corvallis, Oregon

Sweet And Sour Chinese Fish

Serves: 4
Prep Time: 45 minutes

1 **lb. mackerel**	½ **green pepper**
salt and pepper	1 **carrot**
1 **egg**	¼ **cup crushed pineapple**
4 **T. flour**	**dash of Chinese dragon**
1 **can sweet and sour**	**salt**
vegetables	

Skin and bone fish. Season with salt and pepper to taste. Mix egg and flour and dip fish into batter. Deep-fry fish for 5 minutes. Bring sweet and sour vegetables to a boil. Cut pepper and carrot into ¼-inch shreds. Add pineapple, carrot and green pepper to sweet and sour vegetables. Heat and pour over fish. (Or add fish to pot for a few minutes.)

Joanna Headley
Miami, Florida

Steamed Mackerel With Meat

Serves: 5
Prep Time: 25 minutes

1 **lb. mackerel**
4 **large mushrooms**
1 **green onion, cut to desired size**
⅛ **lb. ham or turkey**
3 **T. stir-fry mix**
⅔ **cup water**

Soak dried mushrooms. Remove stems. Slice mushrooms and ham into matchstick-sized shreds. Place fish in heat-proof dish. Combine stir-fry mix with water. Cover fish with all ingredients and steam for 20 minutes.

Joanna Headley
Miami, Florida

Grilled Hawaiian Fish

Serves: 4
Prep Time: 10 minutes

- **4 5-oz. mahi mahi fillets**
- **1 cup pineapple with juice, fresh or canned**
- **1 tsp. cornstarch**
- **½ tsp. crushed red pepper flakes**
- **1 T. fresh cilantro, chopped**
- **1 T. parsley, chopped**

Combine pineapple, cornstarch and red pepper flakes in pan and bring to a boil. Add cilantro and parsley. Grill or broil fish for 3 minutes on each side. Place fish on platter and top with warm sauce. Serve with rice.

Jeannine and Richard Filsinger
Honolulu, Hawaii

Mahi Mahi Magic

Serves: 4-6
Prep Time: 45 minutes

- **4 medium fillets**
- **tomato sauce**
- **green peppers, chopped**
- **onions, chopped**
- **parsley to taste**
- **salt and pepper to taste**

Cut fillets into strips and place in cooking pot. Add tomato sauce, peppers, onions, parsley and salt and pepper. Cook for about 20 minutes. Let simmer for about 5 minutes. Serve.

Oswaldo Tapanes
Miami, Florida

"Kipper's" Fish

Serves: 4
Prep Time: 5 minutes

2 lbs. mahi mahi fillets
⅓ cup soy sauce
⅓ cup lemon juice
⅓ cup oil
   dash of garlic powder
¼ tsp. parsley
   salt and pepper to taste

Combine soy sauce, lemon juice, oil, garlic powder, parsley and salt and pepper. Marinate fillets in mixture overnight. Rub cooking oil on double-thick aluminum foil. Place fish on foil and put on medium-hot barbecue grill, covered. Pour small amount of marinade over fillets. Cook for 12 minutes or until fillets flake. Do not turn.

Edward Knittle
Lakewood, Colorado

Pike Nuggets

Serves: 4-6
Prep Time: 15 minutes

- **3 lbs. pike fillets, cut into 1½-inch cubes**
- **1 large onion, coarsely chopped**
- **2 T. salt**
- **2 cups dry pancake batter**
- **⅛ tsp. Tabasco**
- **1 tsp. dill weed**
  cooking oil

Put pike cubes in large glass bowl. Cover with cold water. Add onion and salt to water and mix into fish. Let stand in refrigerator overnight. Remove fish and rinse with cold water. Make about 2 cups of pancake batter. Add Tabasco and dill weed to batter. Coat fish cubes and deep-fry in oil until done.

Charlie Ladd
Bowling Green, Ohio

Grilled Pike

Serves: 4
Prep Time: 20 minutes

- **4 lbs. pike**
- **2 tsp. butter**
- **1 garlic clove**
- **1 T. onion, minced**
  salt to taste

Place ingredients on fillets. Wrap in aluminum foil and put on grill for 5-7 minutes on each side.

Steve Bumpus
Mason, Michigan

Pike Ala-Mert

Serves: 2
Prep Time: 20 minutes

- **2 pike fillets**
- **1 cup butter**
- **pinch of salt and pepper**
- **1 cup flour**
- **½ cup onion, finely chopped**
- **1 cup fresh mushrooms, sliced**
- **2 lemons**
- **2 tomatoes**
- **¼ cup parsley, chopped**

Melt butter in medium frying pan over medium-high heat. Mix salt, pepper and flour together. Dredge fillets in mixture, then saute in pan for 6 minutes on each side. Remove fillets from pan and set aside. In same pan, put onion and mushrooms and saute until onions are transparent. Add juice from 2 lemons and simmer for 3 minutes. Microwave fillets until hot and place on serving dish. Pour sauce over top. Slice tomatoes and arrange around edge of dish, garnishing with parsley. Serve with wild rice pilaf.

Glenn Strayer
Algona, Iowa

Poor Man's Lobster My Way

Serves: 4
Prep Time: 25 minutes

2 lbs. northern pike fillets
1 gal. water
1 tsp. Mrs. Grass
seasoning salt
1 tsp. Tabasco sauce
butter

Cut fish fillets into 2-inch strips. Bring water to a boil, adding seasoning salt and Tabasco sauce. When water is boiling fast, drop in fish chunks. Bring water to a boil again, then boil for 5 minutes. Take fish from water and place on cooking sheet. Brush with melted butter and sprinkle with seasoning salt. Bake at 350 degrees for a few minutes. Take out and serve with tartar sauce or cocktail sauce.

Brook Kurth
Indianapolis, Indiana

Baked Pike Fillets

Serves: 4
Prep Time: 20 minutes

2 lbs. pike fillets
salt and pepper to taste
flour
2 T. butter, melted

Heat oven to 500 degrees. Season fish with salt and pepper. Place on lightly greased baking pan. Drizzle with butter. Bake uncovered for about 10-15 minutes or until fish flakes easily with a fork.

Douglas Boehmke
Sheridan, Illinois

Fish And Chips

Serves: 5-6
Prep Time: 30 minutes

- **2 lbs. pike fillets**
- **¼ cup milk**
- **⅓ cup Parmesan cheese**
- **1¼ cups potato chips, crushed**
- **½ tsp. salt**
- **¼ tsp. thyme**
- **¼ tsp. pepper**
- **⅓ cup melted butter**

Dip fillets in milk. Combine milk, cheese, chips and spices. Place fillets in buttered 9x13-inch baking dish. Drizzle butter over fillets. Bake at 375 degrees for 22 minutes.

Jeffrey Chmiel
Buffalo, New York

Northern Pike Croquet

Serves: varies
Prep Time: 30 minutes

- **northern pike**
- **onions**
- **green peppers**
- **celery**
- **salt and pepper to taste**
- **bread crumbs**

Put vegetables, seasonings and fillets through blender or meat grinder. Shape mixture into balls. Coat with bread crumbs and deep-fry until done.

William Roe Jr.
Newark, Delaware

Orange Roughy Rollups

Serves: 2
Prep Time: 20-30 minutes

**2-3 orange roughy fillets
mustard
1 cheese slice/fish strip
1 ham slice/fish strip
flour
¼ cup butter
3 T. oil
1 can beer
1½ T. capers**

Cut fillets into 1½ inch strips and cheese and ham into 1-inch strips, spread mustard on fish fillets. Place 1 cheese and ham strip on fish. Roll and tie in both directions with kitchen twine. Roll in flour. Brown in hot butter and oil. Pour in beer. Cover and simmer for 10 minutes. Add capers. Simmer for 10 minutes. Remove string. Serve with rice.

Richard Seymour
Julian, California

Henry's Spicy Roughy

Serves: 1 fillet per person
Prep Time: 15 minutes

**orange roughy fillets
lemon pepper
creole seasoning**

Preheat grill on high setting with lid closed. Put fish on grill basket and season heavily with lemon pepper. Sprinkle creole seasoning to taste. Grill until fish is blackened and serve.

Sam Henry
Ogden, Vermont

Crispy Perch

Serves: 1-2
Prep Time: 5-10 minutes

6 perch fillets
½ tsp. black pepper
½ cup flour
   vegetable oil
   lemon herb seasoning
½ cup butter

1 T. celery, finely minced
1 tsp. garlic, finely minced
1 T. lime juice
½ tsp. salt

Season fish lightly with salt. Dip fish into mixture of pepper and flour. Heat oil to 375 degrees in heavy cast-iron skillet. Fry fish for 2-3 minutes on each side. Pat fish dry on paper towels and keep warm. Season fish lightly with lemon herb seasoning. In separate skillet, melt butter. Add celery, garlic, lime juice and salt. Cook mixture for about 2 minutes. Mixture also makes a great dipping sauce.

Elmer Jensen
Eagle River, Wisconsin

Ginger Ale Perch

Serves: 10
Prep Time: 10 minutes

10 perch fillets
1 can flat ginger ale
1 cup flour
1 large egg
1 tsp. salt

Mix ingredients in large bowl to make light batter. Using deep fryer with hot oil or bacon grease, fry fillets for 3 minutes. Turn and cook until golden brown. Do not overcook.

James Stewart
Inkster, Michigan

Perch Scampi

Serves: 4
Prep Time: 10 minutes

- **1 lb. perch fillets, cut into strips**
- **½ cup butter**
- **½ cup olive oil**
- **¼ cup onion, minced**
- **1 T. garlic, minced**
- **½ cup dry white wine**
- **2 T. lemon juice**
- **4 T. parsley, chopped**
  salt and pepper to taste

In skillet, heat butter and oil. Saute onions and garlic until translucent. Add other ingredients. Pour entire mixture over fillets. In covered dish, microwave on high for 6 minutes.

Conrad Eck
Ellenville, New York

Boiled Perch Fillets

Serves: varies
Prep Time: 30-45 minutes

- **1 lb. perch fillets**
- **1 cup catsup**
- **2 T. horseradish**

Drop fillets in boiling water until meat turns white. Remove from water and bone. Place fish in bowl of ice to cool. Stir catsup and horseradish together for sauce.

Robert Zajkowski Sr.
Hartford, Michigan

Batter-Dipped Perch

Serves: 4 plus (finger snacks)
Prep Time: 2 minutes

> 1½ **lbs. perch fillets**
>   **bacon grease**
> 1 **cup flour**
> ½ **tsp. salt**
> ½ **tsp. garlic powder**
> ½ **tsp. onion powder**
>   **dash of black pepper**
>   **dash of oregano**
>   **dash of paprika**

In large skillet, preheat ¼ inch bacon grease for 2 minutes over medium heat. Mix all dry ingredients. Rinse fillets and dry on paper towels. Add water to mix (making batter to coat spoon, but run off easily.) Add fillets to batter and place in hot grease for 30 seconds. Turn over for 30 seconds. Drain on paper towels. Serve hot. (Do not put in refrigerator.)

Gordon Krise
Harpursville, New York

Baked Perch

Serves: 4
Prep Time: 25 minutes

> 2 **lbs. perch fillets**
>   **salt and pepper to taste**
> 2 **lemons**
> ½ **lb. butter**
> 1 **tsp. parsley**

Season fillets with salt and pepper and arrange three layers in casserole dish. Juice lemons, melt butter and pour mixture over fish. Bake at 325 degrees for 25 minutes. Sprinkle with parsley. Serve with potatoes and salad.

Ron Pasch
Freeport, Illinois

Deep-Fried Perch Fillets

Serves: 4
Prep Time: 30 minutes

- **1 egg**
- **1 cup milk**
- **2 T. barbecue or steak sauce**
- **1 tsp. hot sauce (optional)**
- **1 cup flour**
- **½ tsp seasoned salt**
- **¼ tsp. black pepper**

Mix egg, milk and barbecue or steak sauce together. Mix flour, salt and pepper in paper bag. Dip fish in egg batter, then shake egg-coated fish in bag with flour mixture. Drop floured fish in hot oil until fish float.

Robert Zajkowski Sr.
Hartford, Michigan

Stu Beer-Batter Perch

Serves: 10
Prep Time: 10 minutes

- **10 perch fillets**
- **1 can flat beer**
- **1 cup flour**
- **1 large egg**
- **1 tsp. salt**

Mix ingredients together in large bowl making light batter. Dip fillets in batter, then place in deep-fryer. Cook in hot oil or bacon grease. Let fish cook for 3 minutes, turning when golden brown. For crispy fish, cook a bit longer.

James Stewart
Inkster, Michigan

Redfish In Orange

Serves: 4
Prep Time: 40 minutes

4 redfish fillets
1 egg, beaten
pancake mix
margarine
½ cup orange juice,
fresh-squeezed
1 orange, sliced

Dip fillets into egg, then into pancake mix. Coat lightly. Fry in margarine until lightly browned. Place fried fillets into baking dish. Dribble orange juice over fillets and lay orange slices on top. Cover baking dish and bake at 300 degrees for 30 minutes. Check occasionally, adding more juice as it cooks. Remove cover for last 10 minutes of baking.

Kevin Arrant
Sarasota, Florida

Red Mullet With Cognac

Serves: 4
Prep Time: 30 minutes

- **4 red mullet**
- **2 T. flour**
- **1 T. oil**
- **5 T. butter**
  salt and pepper to taste
- **2 T. cognac**

Clean fish and dust with flour. Fry in hot oil and 1 T. butter for about 10 minutes, turning once. Remove fish and keep warm. Add remaining butter and cognac. Heat thoroughly for 2 minutes and pour over fish.

Joe Tolen
Philadelphia, Pennsylvania

Red Snapper Baked With Oranges And Pineapple

Serves: 2-3
Prep Time: 1 hour

- **2 2-lb. red snappers**
- **3 T. butter**
- **½ cup parsley**
- **⅛ cup pepper**
- **3 T. lemon juice**
- **4 oranges, sliced**
- **½ cup pineapple chunks, semi-drained**

Rub entire fish with butter and place in baking pan. Add parsley and pepper; then drizzle lemon juice over fillets. Lay orange slices and pineapple over top. Bake in oven at 400 degrees for 20 minutes. Reduce temperature to 325 for 20 minutes. Serve on platter or over rice.

Scott Schrauth
Ridgewood, New York

Grilled Red Snapper

Serves: 6
Prep Time: 20-25 minutes

- **6 red snapper fillets**
- **2 T. margarine or butter**
- **½ tsp. paprika**
- **½ tsp. dried oregano**
- **1 garlic clove, crushed**
  dash of ground pepper

Combine butter and seasonings, and brush over fillets. Cover and grill fish about 4 inches from medium coals. Turn fillets occasionally, brushing with seasoned butter. Cook until fish flakes easily.

Mike Sheppard
Escatawapa, Mississippi

Baked Fish In Cheese Sauce

Serves: 4
Prep Time: 40 minutes

1½ lbs. red snapper fillets
3 T. butter or margarine
3 T. flour
1 tsp. salt
½ tsp. dry mustard
¼ tsp. dried dill weed
1½ cups half-and-half
1½ cups cheddar cheese,
shredded
1 4-oz. can mussels,
drained and rinsed or
¼ lb. small shrimp, cooked

Cut fish fillets into serving-sized pieces. Lay fillets in greased, 2-qt. baking dish. In 2-qt. saucepan, melt butter. Stir in flour and cook until bubbly. Add salt, dry mustard and dill. Remove from heat and gradually add half-and-half. Return to heat and cook, stirring constantly until thickened. Add 1 cup cheese, stirring until melted. Add mussels or shrimp. Pour cheese sauce evenly over fish and sprinkle remaining cheese on top. Bake at 400 degrees for 20 minutes or until fish flakes easily with fork.

James Strunk
Philadelphia, Pennsylvania

Oven-Steamed Salmon

Serves: 8
Prep Time: 30 minutes

**1 6-lb. salmon, dressed
with head removed**
½ cup butter, softened
**1 tsp. dried tarragon,
crushed**
**½ tsp. lemon peel, finely
shredded
salt and pepper to taste**
2 lemons, thinly sliced
**2 onions, sliced
fresh parsley or dill**

Combine butter, tarragon and lemon peel; beat well. Cover and chill until serving time. Cover large baking sheet with enough aluminum foil to completely enclose salmon. Place salmon on top. Season salmon cavity with salt and pepper. Mix remaining ingredients. Fill cavity with half of mixture. Layer remaining lemon, onions and herb on top of salmon. Wrap foil tightly around fish. Bake at 325 degrees for 1-2 hours, or until fish is flaky. Serve with lemon-tarragon butter.

Bill Guertner
Eatonville, Washington

Char-Broiled Salmon Steaks

Serves: 1 steak per person
Prep Time: varies

**salmon steaks
Italian dressing**

Soak fillets in Italian dressing for 1-2 hours in refrigerator. Place fish steak on gas or charcoal grill. Cook each side until flaky.

Nelson Wertman
Romulus, New York

Barbecued Salmon

Serves: 4-6
Prep Time: 30 minutes

1 **3-lb. salmon fillet**
   dash of pepper
   lemon herb spice
   pinch of tarragon
¼ **cup butter**
1 **garlic clove, chopped or**
   pressed

Wash salmon and pat dry. Place fish skin-side down on a piece of aluminum foil folded into a "pan." Sandwich in a wire rack. Season with pepper, lemon herb and tarragon. Place fish meat-side down on barbecue grill for 5 minutes. Melt butter and add garlic. Turn salmon and drizzle garlic and butter mixture over fish. Cook for another 10 minutes or until done.

Gordon Monten Jr.
Belfair, Washington

Salmon Ala Foil

Serves: varies
Prep Time: 30-45 minutes

1 **8-lb. salmon**
   butter
   lemon juice
   garlic, crushed
   seasoning salt
1 **celery stalk, chopped**
1 **onion, chopped**

Mix butter, lemon juice, garlic, seasoning salt, celery and onion. Wrap mixture in aluminum foil with fish. Bake for 30-45 minutes at 350 degrees, or on low heat on barbecue grill.

Delbert Thompson
Woodland, Washington

Salmon Stuffing

Serves: 4
Prep Time: 30 minutes

1 3-lb. salmon
½ cup onion, diced
½ cup celery, diced
⅓ cup green pepper, diced
¼ cup butter
1 tsp. parsley
3 cups canned tomatoes, drained
½ tsp. Tabasco sauce
1½ tsp. MSG
1½ tsp. salt
1½ tsp. garlic salt
pinch of thyme
1½ cups rice, cooked

Saute onion, celery and green pepper in butter. Stir in parsley. Add tomatoes, Tabasco sauce, MSG, salt, garlic salt, thyme and rice, mixing thoroughly. Stuff salmon with mixture and cover. Bake at 400 degrees for 10 minutes. Reduce heat to 350 degrees and continue baking for 50 minutes or until done.

James Sontag
Pocatello, Idaho

Baked Salmon

Serves: 4
Prep Time: 30 minutes

4 salmon steaks
1 cup milk
1 cup mayonnaise
4 medium potatoes, cubed
1 small onion, sliced
salt and pepper to taste

Combine milk and mayonnaise. Put salmon steaks, potatoes and onion slices in casserole dish. Cover with milk and mayonnaise mixture. Season with salt and pepper. Bake at 350 degrees for 1 hour, 30 minutes.

Milbert Schaffer
Pierre, South Dakota

Crispy Salmon Steaks

Serves: 6
Prep Time: 45 minutes

6 salmon steaks	**1 cup crackers, crushed**
½ cup butter or	**1 cup potato chips,**
margarine, melted	**crushed**
1 tsp. salt	**6 lemon wedges**
⅛ tsp. paprika	**6 parsley sprigs**

Combine butter, salt and paprika. In separate bowl, combine crackers and potato chips. Wipe steaks with damp cloth. Dip steaks into butter mixture, then cracker mixture. Arrange steaks on lightly greased broiler pan and place on rack. Broil 6 inches from heat for 5-8 minutes. Turn steaks and broil another 5-8 minutes or until fish flakes easily with fork. Serve each steak with lemon wedge and parsley sprig.

Scott Chastain
Haines City, Florida

Basic Canned Fish

Serves: makes 1 quart
Prep Time: 5 hours

salmon
onions, sliced
1 tsp. canning salt
1 T. white vinegar
1 T. catsup
1 T. cooking oil

Cut fish into 1- to 2-inch strips. Then pack fish in 1-qt. jar, alternating with fish and onions. Put salt, vinegar, catsup and oil on top of fish. Seal jar. Cold pack for 4-5 hours or 90 minutes in pressure cooker.

William Rottler
Fountain, Michigan

Broiled Salmon Steaks

Serves: 4
Prep Time: 25 minutes

4 12-oz. coho salmon steaks	1 T. ground cloves
½ cup olive oil	⅛ cup dry white wine
1 tsp. dill weed, dried	¼ cup soy sauce
¼ cup lemon juice	1 tsp. pepper
	fresh parsley (optional)

Combine olive oil, dill weed, lemon juice, cloves, wine and soy sauce in saucepan; mix well. Place steaks in pan; turn to marinate both sides. Place steaks on baking sheet and brush steaks once again before broiling. Broil steaks on both sides for about 5-7 minutes. (Do not overcook.) Remove from broiler. Sprinkle sparingly with fresh parsley. Serve immediately.

Christopher Marino
Staten Island, New York

Great Lakes Canned Salmon

Serves: 3-4
Prep Time: 1 hour, 30 minutes

    salmon fillets
1 pt.-sized jar and lid
1 T. Thousand Island
    salad dressing
½ tsp. canning salt
1 T. white vinegar
½ tsp. seasoning salt

Cut salmon fillets into 1½-inch chunks. Pack jar with salmon, draining any excess water. Combine remaining ingredients and add to jar. Firmly tighten lid on jar. Cook jar in pressure cooker for 90 minutes at 10-lbs. pressure.

Bob Trnka
Waseca, Minnesota

Baked Salmon Dijon

Serves: 4
Prep Time: 10 minutes

4½ lbs. salmon fillets
2 T. butter, melted
½ cup mayonnaise
2 T. Dijon mustard
3 T. grated Parmesan
cheese
ground black pepper to
taste

Rinse fillets and pat dry. Cover pan with aluminum foil. Place fillets skin-side up on pan and brush 1 T. melted butter over them. Broil for 4 minutes, and turn fillets over. Brush with remaining butter. Broil 4 more minutes. While fish broils, combine mayonnaise, mustard, Parmesan cheese and pepper. Brush fish pieces with mayonnaise mixture. Return to broiler. Broil for 3-4 minutes until fish flakes easily and topping is golden brown.

Michael Berge
North Bend, Oregon

Baked Salmon Hash

Serves: 2
Prep Time: 1 hour

1 lb. salmon
1½ cups potatoes, diced
and cooked
1½ cups onion, diced
½ tsp. salt
⅛ tsp. paprika

Combine ingredients. Place mixture into oiled baking pan and bake at 350 degrees for 1 hour.

Joe Buckles
Michigan Center, Michigan

Savory Grilled Salmon

Serves: 4-6
Prep Time: 10-15 minutes

salmon fillets	**lemon juice**
¼ tsp. pepper	**2 bacon strips**
2 garlic cloves, minced	**mushrooms, sliced**
¼ tsp. garlic salt	**onion, sliced (optional)**
4 pats butter	

Use enough aluminum foil to fold over fish forming a tent. Sprinkle pepper, garlic, garlic salt and butter on top of fish. Drizzle lemon juice over fish and add bacon strips. Cover fish completely with mushrooms. Add onion if desired. Fold foil over fish and seal. Cook on barbecue grill for 25-30 minutes.

Gary Moore
Eltopia, Washington

Salmon Patties

Serves: varies
Prep Time: 30 minutes

- **3 cups salmon, cooked**
- **1½ cups bread crumbs**
- **½ cup onions, diced**
- **½ cup green peppers, diced**
- **instant potato flakes**
- **2 pinches of cayenne**
- **cooking oil**
- **butter or margarine**

Mix salmon, bread crumbs, onions and green peppers. Form mixture into patties and dip in potato flakes mixed with cayenne. Fry in mix of hot oil and butter or margarine until patties are golden brown.

Mark Siack
Eureka, California

Salmon Continental

Serves: 4-6
Prep Time: 30-45 minutes

4-6 salmon fillets
  ½ cup clarified butter
  ¼ cup dry vermouth
     seasoning salt
     paprika
     lemon wedges
     parsley flakes

Lightly brush both sides of salmon fillets with butter and vermouth mixture. Place fish on grill over moderate heat. Sprinkle seasoning salt and paprika on fillets. Cook until first side is firm. Turn fillets and repeat procedure. (Be sure to cover grill between turns.) Before removing from grill, drizzle lemon juice and sprinkle parsley over fillets. (It can be broiled in oven, also.)

Chris Seung
Mukilteo, Washington

Grilled Salmon

Serves: 3
Prep Time: 15 minutes

  3 lbs. fish
  ½ stick butter
     seafood seasoning
  ½ tsp. garlic powder
  ¾ tsp. seasoning salt
  ¼ tsp. lemon pepper

Combine butter and seasonings. Baste fish on one side and cook for 7 minutes; turn and cook for an additional 7 minutes.

Chad Martin
Redwood Falls, Minnesota

Smoked Fish Dutches

Serves: varies
Prep Time: 15-20 minutes

- **1 cup smoked salmon**
- **½ cup butter**
- **⅛ cup salt**
- **1 cup boiling water**
- **1 cup flour, sifted**
- **3 eggs, unbeaten**
- **1 8-oz. pkg. cream cheese**
- **⅛ cup dried onion**
- **¼ cup celery, minced**
- **1 T. lemon juice**
- **paprika**
- **salt to taste**
- **garlic powder to taste**

Add butter and salt to boiling water. Stir over medium heat until mixture boils. Reduce heat and add flour. Beat until mixture leaves sides of pan. Remove from heat and add one egg at a time, beating thoroughly after each addition. Shape by teaspoons into small puffs. Bake at 450 degrees for about 8 minutes or until points turn brown. Reduce heat to 350 and bake for 10-20 minutes. Meanwhile combine remaining ingredients to make filling. Cut small slit on one side and stuff with filling.

Barbara Mills
Clinton, Washington

Salmon Gourmet

Serves: 4
Prep Time: 35-40 minutes

1 **lb. salmon fillet, flaked**
4 **potatoes, cooked**
  butter
  milk
  salt and pepper
½ **cup Swiss cheese, grated**

1 **egg yolk**
1 **cup medium white sauce**
  buttered bread crumbs

Mash potatoes with butter, milk and seasoning in amounts desired. Line greased baking dish with potatoes. Add cheese and egg yolk to white sauce and pour half of mixture over potatoes. Add fish to baking dish, cover with remaining sauce and top with bread crumbs. Bake at 350 degrees for 20 minutes.

Traci Nagy
Cuyahoga Falls, Ohio

Smoked Salmon Spread

Serves: 8-12
Prep Time: 20-30 minutes

5 **oz. smoked salmon, minced**
8 **oz. cream cheese, softened**
3 **T. heavy whipping cream**
1 **T. fresh chives or green onions, minced**

fresh squeezed lemon juice
ground cayenne pepper to taste
fresh ground black pepper to taste

Combine cheese and cream in bowl. Whip with mixer until fluffy. Stir in smoked salmon, chives, lemon juice, cayenne pepper and black pepper.

James Cepress
Roseville, Minnesota

Salmon Chowder

Serves: 8
Prep Time: 45 minutes

1 lb. salmon, bones and
skin removed
1 medium onion, chopped
4 T. butter or margarine
1 cup water
1 20-oz. pkg. frozen
chopped broccoli
2 tsp. instant chicken
bouillon

1 14½-oz. can evaporated
milk
2 T. flour
4 cups milk
salt to taste
white pepper to taste

In Dutch oven saute onion in butter until transparent. Add water and broccoli. Simmer until broccoli is tender. Mix salmon, bouillon, evaporated milk, flour and milk. Season with salt and pepper to taste. Heat until mixture thickens slightly.

Mark Schmaltz
Niles, Michigan

Grilled Fennel-Stuffed Salmon

Serves: 4
Prep Time: 20-30 minutes

4 small whole salmon
salt and pepper to taste
1 sweet fennel bulb,
thinly sliced (vertical)
2 lemons, thinly sliced
olive oil

Heat charcoal in uncovered grill. Rinse salmon in cold water and pat dry. Season lightly with salt and pepper. Stuff fish cavities with fennel and lemon slices. Brush fish all over with olive oil. Grill. Turn over once. Cook for about 10 minutes.

James Cepress
Roseville, Minnesota

Barbecued Salmon

Serves: 4
Prep Time: 5 hours

1½ **lbs. salmon steaks, 1**
   inch thick
3 **T. dry white wine**
3 **T. soy sauce**
2 **T. dark brown sugar,**
   firmly packed

1 **T. sesame oil**
1 **large bunch spinach,**
   stemmed
1 **can pineapple chunks**

Combine wine, soy sauce, sugar and oil to make marinade.
When sugar melts, pour marinade over salmon steaks. Cover
and refrigerate for at least 3 hours, turning occasionally.
Prepare barbecue grill. Grease rack. Drain salmon. (Save
marinade.) Put fish on grill and cook until meat is opaque,
about 9 minutes per inch, turning once. Simmer reserved
marinade until reduced to 4 tablespoons. Transfer fish to
spinach-lined platter. Spoon marinade over fish and garnish
with pineapple.

Paul Grimes
Rio Rancho, New Mexico

Salmon Balls In Mushroom Sauce

Serves: 4
Prep Time: 45 minutes

1 **lb. salmon**
1 **cup rice, cooked**
2 **eggs, slightly beaten**
1 **tsp. onion, minced**
1 **tsp. salt**

½ **cup bread crumbs**
1 **can cream of mushroom**
   soup
½ **cup water**
2 **green peppers, chopped**

Mix salmon, rice, eggs, onion, salt and bread crumbs together
and form into balls. Combine soup, water and green pepper
and pour into casserole dish. Drop salmon balls into dish and
bake at 350 degrees for 30 minutes.

Ed Kowalski
Chicago, Illinois

John's Grilled Salmon

Serves: 6
Prep Time: 20 minutes

- **2 lbs. fish fillets**
- **2 tsp. lemon juice**
  salt and pepper to taste
  seasoning salt
- **¼ stick butter**

Place fish fillets in fish basket or rack. Season lightly with salt, pepper and seasoning salt on both sides. If using gas grill, set on medium heat. Place fish on grill, baste fillet tops and cover for about 2 minutes. Turn fish over and baste again. Repeat procedure until fish is completely cooked.

John William Wicke
Frankfort, Michigan

Pepper Grilled Salmon

Serves: 4
Prep Time: 30 minutes

- **1 15-oz. salmon fillet**
- **1 tsp. black peppercorns**
- **1 tsp. anise seeds**
- **½ tsp. course kosher salt**

Spray grill rack with non-stick cooking spray. Place rack 5 inches from coals. In blender, spice mill or with mortar and pestle, grind peppercorns, anise seeds and salt until coarse; sprinkle mixture over salmon. Grill salmon for 4-5 minutes on each side or until thoroughly cooked.

James Hodgdon
Kansas City, Missouri

Salmon Soup

Serves: 6 or more
Prep Time: 10 minutes

> **fresh salmon**
> **4 cups milk**
> **½ cup cider vinegar**
> **½ stick butter**
> **salt and pepper to taste**

Simmer milk in saucepan. (Do not bring to a boil.) Add boneless salmon. Slowly stir in cider vinegar and add butter; let melt. Season with salt and pepper and simmer. (Do not boil mixture.) Serve with oyster crackers or grilled cheese sandwiches.

Ricky Kirk
Las Vegas, Nevada

Jerked Salmon

Serves: 4-6
Prep Time: 2 days

> **10 lbs. salmon fillets**
> **4 T. sugar**
> **1 cup sea salt or**
> **non-iodized salt**
> **2 qts. water**

Dissolve sugar and salt in water to make brine. Marinate salmon fillets in brine for 12 hours in refrigerator. Remove and pat dry. Smoke fish in smoker for 10-12 hours or until fish is hard and stiff.

T. J. Brant
Olympia, Washington

Dry Mix For Smoked Salmon

Serves: varies
Prep Time: 6 hours

> **salmon fillets**
> 1 **cup brown sugar**
> 1 **cup white sugar**
> ½ **cup salt**
> 1 **tsp. garlic salt**
> 1 **tsp. black pepper**
> 1 **part honey**
> 1 **part water**

Mix sugars, salts and pepper in plastic bag. Add thin salmon fillets, coating well. Lay coated fish on rack or cookie sheet to drain for 2 hours. Arrange fillets on rack in smoker and smoke for 4 hours. An hour before taking from smoker, baste (spray bottle) with 1 part honey and 1 part water for glaze.

Gary Belshe
Lakeside, Oregon

Smoked Salmon

Serves: 3-4
Prep Time: overnight plus 1 hour

> **salmon fillets or 1-inch**
> **steaks**
> **salt to taste**
> 1 **lb. brown sugar**

Generously season fish with salt. Pack fish between layers of brown sugar. Set overnight. Rinse fish in resulting liquid. Smoke with your favorite chips until desired consistency is reached or until firm. Remove. Cool in refrigerator.

Barbara Mills
Clinton, Washington

Kipper Morning

Serves: 2
Prep Time: 45 minutes

- **2 salmon fillets, halved**
- **3 garlic cloves, chopped**
- **½ cup olive oil**
- **¼ tsp. dried parsley**
- **½ tsp. salt**
- **2 eggs**

In large frying pan, saute garlic on low heat with dried parsley and salt in olive oil. Place fillets in pan and cook until flaky. Place egg on every other fillet, then cover and let eggs cook.

Robert Schneiderman
Flushing, New York

Baked Salmon Steaks

Serves: 4
Prep Time: 30 minutes

- **4 1-inch salmon steaks**
- **¼ cup butter, melted**
- **½ tsp. salt**
- **¼ tsp. paprika**
- **2 T. barbecue sauce**
- **1 tsp. Worcestershire sauce**
- **lemon juice**

Put salmon steaks in shallow baking dish. In separate pan, melt butter. Add salt, paprika, barbecue sauce and Worcestershire sauce. Brush mixture over each steak, then lightly drizzle with lemon juice. Bake at 375 degrees for about 20-25 minutes.

Tom Ruhl
Princeton, Wisconsin

Seafood Omelet

Serves: 2
Prep Time: 20 minutes

- 1 **2-oz. smoked salmon, chunked**
- 4 **eggs**
- 2 **T. water**
- 1 **small can mushrooms, sliced**
- 1-2 **oz. shrimp, chopped and cooked**
- 2 **oz. cheese, shredded salt and lemon pepper to taste**

Beat eggs in bowl with water. Pour eggs in hot, oiled skillet and cook eggs until almost firm. Spread mushrooms, shrimp, cheese and salt and pepper over half of omelet. Slide omelet from pan with seafood-side first and flip top over.

Joe Gerencser Jr.
Milford, Indiana

Salmon On The Grill

Serves: 4
Prep Time: 35 minutes

- 1 **salmon fillet**
- 1 **lemon seasoning salt garlic fresh ground pepper**

Wash fish thoroughly and pat dry. Rub fish with fresh lemon. Sprinkle seasoning salt, garlic and fresh ground pepper over fish. Grill for 30 minutes or until fish is tender.

Nate Gadzik
Mesa, Arizona

Canned Smoked Salmon

Serves: varies
Prep Time: 8 hours

> **salmon fillets**
> **salt to taste**
> **water**

In large granite, plastic or crock container, soak fish fillets with salt water or brine overnight. Remove from brine, drain or pat dry. Arrange on rack in smoker and smoke for 5-6 hours. Place in pint canning jars with no liquid or salt added. Process in pressure cooker for 105 minutes at 10-lbs. pressure.

Gary Belshe
Lakeside, Oregon

Salmon Dip

Serves: varies
Prep Time: 3 hours

> 1 **lb. salmon**
> 8 **oz. cream cheese**
> 1 **small green onion,**
> **chopped**
> 1 **tsp. lemon juice**
> ½ **tsp. salt**
> ⅛ **tsp. pepper**
> ⅛ **tsp. dill**
> 2 **T. capers**

Blend ingredients together at medium speed until smooth. Pour mixture into small bowl, and stir in capers. Cover bowl and chill for 2-3 hours. Serve on crackers or use as dip for chips.

Kenneth Posseneau
Wisconsin Rapids, Wisconsin

Shark Brochettes

Serves: 4-6
Prep Time: 1 hour, 30 minutes

1 **lb. shark steak**
¼ **cup soy sauce**
¼ **cup dry white wine**
¼ **cup Worcestershire sauce**
2 **T. olive oil**

8 **oz. small mushrooms**
1 **small green pepper, chopped**
1 **small red bell pepper, chopped**

In large bowl, mix liquids. Wash and pat dry fish and cut into 1-inch squares. Add fish to liquid mixture, cover and refrigerate for 1 hour. Shake every 10 minutes. Remove from refrigerator and thread onto small skewers, alternating shark, mushrooms and peppers. Arrange on medium-hot barbecue grill, approximately 3 inches apart. Brush reserved marinade onto skewers. Turn only once when grilling. Fish is done when lightly brown, about 10-15 minutes.

Todd Streit
Pasadena, California

Shark Fillets

Serves: 4
Prep Time: 20 minutes

4 **shark fillets**
   pepper to taste
   garlic powder to taste
   lemon juice
4-7 **T. butter**

Season fillets with pepper and garlic powder and place in shallow pan. Cover with lemon juice or marinate overnight. Wrap fillets in aluminum foil. Put butter on top of fillets. Heat oven or grill to 350 degrees and bake for 20-25 minutes.

Leo Dunn
Park Forest, Illinois

Breakfast Baked Snook

Serves: 2-4
Prep Time: 15 minutes

- **2 snook fillets, ½ inch thick**
- **2 tsp. salt**
- **½ cup milk**
- **1½ cups cornflakes, slightly crushed**
- **2 T. butter, melted**

Dissolve salt into milk, then mix with cornflakes. Add fillets and butter. Bake on greased cookie sheet for about 20 minutes at 400 degrees.

Art Harris
Jupiter, Florida

Baked Sole With Broccoli

Serves: 4
Prep Time: 30-35 minutes

2 lbs. sole fillets	**salted water**
½ tsp. salt	**3 T. butter or margarine**
dash of white pepper	**3 T. fresh lemon juice**
dash of paprika	**¾ cup sour cream**
1 10-oz. pkg. frozen	**3-4 lemon pieces, thinly**
broccoli spears	**sliced**

Sprinkle seasonings over fillets. Boil broccoli for 4 minutes; drain. Arrange broccoli in lightly buttered baking dish. Place fish fillets, folded in halves, on top. Dot fillets with butter and drizzle with lemon juice. Cover with foil; bake at 350 degrees for 20-25 minutes. Pour liquid off fish. Add 3-4 T. liquid to sour cream for sauce. Add lemon pieces.

James Strunk
Philadelphia, Pennsylvania

Nordick Stuffed Fillet Ala Lisa

Serves: 4
Prep Time: 45 minutes

6 sole fillets	**1½ cups Monterey Jack**
1 cup mushrooms	**cheese, shredded**
⅓ cup broccoli florets	**1 tsp. olive oil**
1 small onion, chopped	**salt and pepper to taste**
2 T. butter	**paprika**
¼ cup bread crumbs	**lemon juice**

Brown mushrooms, broccoli and onion in butter. Remove from heat. Stir in bread crumbs and 1 cup cheese. Rub olive oil on fillets. Place dollop of broccoli mixture in middle of fillets. Roll fillets up and secure with toothpicks, seam-side down. Sprinkle seasonings over fish. Drizzle with lemon juice and cover with remaining cheese. Bake for 20 minutes at 375 degrees.

Lisa Sinclair
Salem, New Jersey

Baked Striped Bass With Clams

Serves: 8
Prep Time: 40-50 minutes

4 lbs. striped bass
12 hard-shelled clams
1 tsp. salt
¼ tsp. basil
dash of pepper
½ cup parsley sprigs
1 medium onion, thinly sliced

2 celery stalks with leaves, chopped
1 garlic clove, halved
2 bay leaves
½ cup dry white wine
½ cup butter or margarine, melted

Dress and bone fish leaving head on. Preheat oven to 350 degrees 1 hour prior to serving. Grease large, shallow baking pan or ovenproof serving dish. Scrub clams under running cold water; set aside. Season inside of fish with salt, basil and pepper. Arrange parsley and half of onion slices inside fish; place fish in pan. Arrange clams, remaining onion, celery, garlic and bay leaves around fish. Pour wine and butter over fish. Cover pan with aluminum foil and bake for 40-50 minutes until fish flakes easily with fork and clam shells open. Discard garlic and bay leaves. Carve fish into portions and serve.

John Wirth
Plainview, New York

Marinated Grilled Striper

Serves: varies
Prep Time: 10 minutes

striper fillets
your favorite Italian dressing

Cut striper fillets into 4-inch squares. Place fish in dish and pour dressing over fish. Refrigerate for 1-2 hours. Grill on charcoal until done. Baste fish with dressing while grilling.

Bill Henley Jr.
Hopewell, Virginia

Striped Fish Supreme

Serves: 4-6
Prep Time: 2 hours

1 **large striper**	2 **tsp. Old Bay seasoning**
2 **large eggs**	**sweet basil**
1-2 **pts. crabmeat**	**oregano**
bread crumbs	**salt and pepper**
Worcestershire sauce	**lemon wedges**

Partially sew fish stomachs with white thread. Lightly beat eggs and add crabmeat, bread crumbs, Worcestershire sauce and Old Bay seasoning; knead mixture. Stuff mixture into bass and complete sewing process. Lay fish on two sheets of aluminum foil. Season lightly .with Old Bay, sweet basil, oregano and salt and pepper. Add lemon wedges and seal foil. Place foil on baking sheet and cook for 90 minutes at 400 degrees.

James Eastridge
North East, Maryland

Striper Deep-Fry

Serves: 4-5
Prep Time: 1 hour

6 **striper fillets**	2 **T. pepper**
4 **cups flour**	1 **egg**
3 **cups cornmeal**	1½ **cups milk**
4 **T. garlic salt**	**peanut oil**
2 **T. salt**	

Cut each fillet into 2-3 pieces. Combine dry ingredients in bag. Shake bag until well mixed. In medium bowl, beat egg thoroughly. Add milk to egg and mix. Place 8 pieces of fish into egg-milk mixture, then place in flour bag, coating well. Heat peanut oil in large heavy fryer. Lightly brown fillets (2-4 minutes), then place on paper towels. Lightly salt fish. Repeat.

Mildred Jackson
Williston, South Carolina

Beer Batter Sturgeon

Serves: varies
Prep Time: 8-12 minutes

sturgeon
oil
salt and pepper to taste
your favorite beer
flour
lemon wedges

Heat oil in deep-fat fryer. Cut sturgeon into bite-sized chunks.
Season chunks with salt and pepper. Mix beer and flour.
Dredge fish in mixture, covering thoroughly. Place battered fish
into oil and deep-fry until golden brown; remove. Serve with
lemon wedges.

Jeff Dominquez
Vacaville, California

Orange And Basil Marinated Swordfish

Serves: 1
Prep Time: 55 minutes

1 10-oz. swordfish steak	salt to taste
3 oranges	freshly ground black
3 lemons	pepper to taste
10 fresh basil leaves	grilled vegetables
1 T. olive oil	dill rice

Squeeze juice from oranges and lemons, straining seeds.
Combine basil, orange juice, lemon juice and olive oil in
baking dish. Rinse steaks with cold water. Pat dry and season
both sides generously with salt and pepper. Place swordfish
steaks in baking dish and marinate for approximately 45
minutes. Grill on medium heat (325-350 degrees) for
approximately 4 minutes per side, or until fish is opaque. Serve
with lemon, orange slices, your favorite grilled vegetables and
dill rice.

John Wirth
Plainview, New York

Zesty Tomato Fillets

Serves: 4
Prep Time: 20 minutes

1 lb. swordfish fillets	¼ cup carrots, chopped
½ cup green pepper, chopped	1 8-oz. can tomatoes, chopped
¼ cup onion, chopped	1 tsp. chicken bouillon
¼ cup celery, chopped	⅛ tsp. cayenne pepper

Combine green pepper, onion, celery, carrots, tomatoes,
bouillon and pepper in 8-inch microwave baking dish. Arrange
fillets on top, folding edges. Cover and microwave on high
power for 6-7 minutes or until fish flakes easily with fork.

Donald Kimberling
Omaha, Nebraska

Baked Stuffed Trout

Serves: 4
Prep Time: 1 hour, 15 minutes

4 trout (2 large, 2 small)	**¼ cup onion, grated**
1 onion, sliced	**2 eggs**
2 T. vinegar	**1 T. mayonnaise**
1 lemon	**salt and pepper**
1 can crabmeat	**2 bacon strips**
½ cup celery, grated	**2 T. butter or margarine**
½ cup carrots, grated	

Put small trout in pot of water. Add sliced onion and vinegar and half of lemon. Cook until skin comes off easily and remove bones. In large bowl, add cooked trout and crabmeat. Then, add grated celery, carrots, onion, eggs and mayonnaise. Season to taste with salt and pepper. Mix well and stuff into large trout. Wrap 1 bacon strip around each trout, place on aluminum foil, adding butter or margarine to each. Then wrap trout individually. Bake at 350 degrees for approximately 1 hour.

Leo Wiskirski
Summit Hill, Pennsylvania

Pan-Fried Trout

Serves: 4
Prep Time: 5 minutes

4 trout fillets
1 egg, beaten
instant mashed potatoes
cooking oil

Dip fillets in egg, then in potato buds. Fry in oil until brown.

Charles Everts
Ogden, Utah

Baked Trout With Cheese

Serves: 2
Prep Time: 30-40 minutes

1 lb. trout fillets, skins removed	1 large onion, diced
6 oz. American cheese	1 garlic clove, minced
¼ cup fresh parsley, chopped	2 T. flour
1 tsp. oregano, chopped	⅛ tsp. salt
¼ cup olive oil	⅛ tsp. pepper
	1½ cups milk
	1 tsp. lemon juice

Alternate layers of fish and cheese in greased, glass baking dish (end with cheese on top). Sprinkle parsley and oregano over fish. Heat olive oil in skillet and saute onion and garlic until tender, stirring constantly. Stir in flour, salt and pepper. Gradually add milk, stirring constantly. Cook until thickened and pour over fish and cheese. Bake at 400 degrees for about 20-30 minutes or until fish flakes easily. Drizzle with lemon juice and serve immediately.

Susan Cook
Holcomb, New York

Deep-Fried Sea Trout

Serves: 4
Prep Time: 15 minutes

trout fillets	1-2 T. cinnamon
salt and pepper	1 can beer
1 cup flour	1 tsp. paprika
1 tsp. pepper	cooking oil

Season fillets with salt and pepper to taste. Combine flour, pepper, cinnamon, beer and paprika, making light batter. Roll fillets in batter. Heat cooking oil to 450 degrees. Drop fillets in oil. Cook until golden brown.

Leo Dunn
Park Forest, Illinois

Lakeside Trout

Serves: 2
Prep Time: 30-45 minutes

4 trout
2 T. butter
¼ cup lemon juice
½ tsp. garlic powder

½ tsp. hickory salt
4 lemon slices, halved
¼ tsp. pepper

Cut heads and tails off trout. Slice trout (belly) from gills to vent. Gut trout. (Do not disturb bones.) Melt butter in large skillet over low flame. Add ⅛ cup lemon juice and garlic powder. Sprinkle hickory salt on trout (inside). Place 1 lemon slice in each trout. Cook trout on medium flame or coals until skin begins to separate from flesh, 3-5 minutes each side or until flaky. Remove trout from pan. Gently peel skin and carefully separate meat from bone with fork by working from backbone to belly. You should end up with a full rib cage and boneless trout. Season with remaining lemon juice, hickory salt and pepper.

Walt Lepak
Meriden, Connecticut

All There Is, Trout

Serves: 2
Prep Time: 45 minutes

rainbow trout fillets,
pan-dressed
12 oz. dry ginger ale
½ cup flour

salt and pepper to taste
1 lemon, thinly sliced
1 T. butter
2 T. oil

Marinate trout in ginger ale for 30 minutes. Dredge trout in flour and salt and pepper. Place lemon slices in body cavity. Heat butter and oil in heavy skillet. Panfry trout for 5 minutes per side.

S. Douglas
Roslindale, Massachusetts

Bacon Lakers

Serves: 4
Prep Time: 1 hour

2 lake trout, 20-26 inches
4 bacon strips
½ stick butter
lemon pepper to taste

Preheat oven to 400 degrees. Place bacon strips in rib cavity of each trout. Smear half of butter around bacon. Season bacon and butter heavily with lemon pepper. Wrap fillets in aluminum foil and seal loosely. Place in large rectangular baking dish and bake for 45 minutes. Remove pan from oven and open foil. With knife, cut along fish's lateral line from head to tail down to backbone. Remove skin and meat from bone. Peel backbone from lower half of meat, remove skin. Place meat and bacon on plate. Serve.

Richard Rooney
Laramie, Wyoming

Baked Rainbow Trout

Serves: varies
Prep Time: 30-45 minutes

rainbow trout
1 stick butter
½ cup lemon juice
onions to taste, chopped
salt to taste
garlic to taste, minced

Melt butter and mix with lemon juice. Spoon mixture over split fish. Put onion, salt and garlic on fish. Wrap fish in aluminum foil. Place in oven or on grill at 300-400 degrees and cook for 30-40 minutes. Spoon more butter and lemon juice on fish before serving.

Patricia McKinney
Carthage, Missouri

Barbecued Trout

Serves: 4-6
Prep Time: 2 hours, 15 minutes

2 lbs. trout fillets, skinned	**dash of Tabasco sauce**
⅓ cup olive oil	**dash of cayenne pepper**
1 T. Worcestershire sauce	**1 large onion, thinly**
1 T. prepared mustard	**sliced**
2 T. brown sugar, packed	**½ tsp. paprika**
1 tsp. salt (optional)	**1 garlic clove, minced**
¾ cup catsup	

Combine all ingredients except fish and mix thoroughly. Wash and dry fillets. Marinate fillets in mixture for at least 2 hours before cooking. Turn fillets often in marinade. Place fillets on lower rack of oven. Bake at 450 degrees for 10 minutes, basting twice. Add water if fillets become too dry. Brown fillets a few minutes under broiler just before serving.

Susan Cook
Holcomb, New York

Broiled Brown Trout

Serves: varies
Prep Time: 30 minutes

**brown trout, filleted and
butterflied
salt and pepper to taste
fresh garlic, minced
butter
onions (optional)
lemon juice**

Preheat broiler. Season fish with salt and pepper. Then add garlic, butter and onion. Place fillets on broiler pan and broil for 5-7 minutes per inch of thickness at about 6 inches from heat source. Add lemon juice and enjoy.

Jerry Gray
Jackson, Wyoming

Lake Trout Ala Lemon-Beer

Serves: 4
Prep Time: 45 minutes

2 lake trout fillets
1 can beer
flour
garlic salt to taste
pepper to taste
vegetable oil
1 lemon

Fill half of baking dish with beer. Soak fillets in beer for 15 minutes. Prepare batter by mixing flour, garlic salt and pepper. When done soaking, pat fish dry. Then, roll fillets in flour mixture. In 10½- or 12-inch skillet, preheat oil so when a ball of flour is dropped, it sizzles. Fry fillets for 5 minutes on each side until fish flakes and batter is golden brown. Squeeze lemon over fish and serve.

David Rose
Traverse City, Minnesota

Grilled Trout

Serves: varies
Prep Time: 15 minutes

trout fillets
butter
lemon pepper seasoning
to taste
bacon strips (optional)

Clean fillets and pat dry. Butter both sides of fillets and sprinkle with lemon pepper seasoning. Wrap bacon strips around fillets. Then, wrap in aluminum foil and cook on grill for 5-6 minutes per side.

Mark Dodson
Corrales, New Mexico

Southern-Fried Trout

Serves: 3-4
Prep Time: 30 minutes

6-8 trout
⅔ cup flour
2 eggs, beaten
½ lb. grease

salt to taste
1 tsp. lemon juice
4 drops Worcestershire
sauce

Clean trout and dredge in flour. In shallow bowl, beat eggs until frothy. Dip floured fish into eggs, coating both sides. In large, heavy skillet, fry fish in hot grease. When almost half done, salt lightly and add lemon juice and Worcestershire sauce. Turn fish over and reduce heat to low, frying for about 15 more minutes. Serve with French-fried onion rings and hushpuppies or corn bread.

Susan Cook
Holcomb, New York

Jeff's Barbecued Trout

Serves: 2
Prep Time: 15 minutes

fresh trout, cleaned
butter
lemon or lime juice
pepper to taste
cooking oil
paprika

Melt butter and mix with lemon juice. Season fillets with pepper. Oil grill thoroughly to keep fish from sticking. Place trout on grill and turn often to keep from curling. Baste with butter mixture. Cook until brown. After basting, sprinkle with paprika.

Jeff Dominquez
Vacaville, California

Smoked Trout

Serves: 20
Prep Time: 8 hours

10 lbs. trout
2 gal. water
½ lb. brown sugar
¾ cup lemon juice
1 tsp. liquid garlic
1 tsp. liquid onion
2 lbs. salt

Clean and split trout lengthwise. Mix remaining ingredients until dissolved. Soak trout for 8 hours in solution. Remove and rinse lightly in clean water. Let air-dry in cool place for 3 hours. Smoke at 80 degrees for 1 hour. Turn heat to 150 degrees in smoker and lightly smoke for 2 hours or until fish flakes easily. Serve hot or cold.

Daniel Wood
Pringle, South Dakota

Pan-Fried Brook Trout

Serves: 2-3 trout per person
Prep Time: 15-20 minutes

brook trout
½ cup flour
½ cup cornmeal
salt to taste
butter or oil

Combine flour, cornmeal and salt. Dredge trout in dry mixture. Melt butter or oil in frying pan. Fry trout at medium heat, turning once.

Edwin Loberg
Annandale, Virginia

Pepper Trout

Serves: 6
Prep Time: 30 minutes

3 lbs. trout fillets	**2 tomatoes, chopped**
2 green peppers, chopped	**2 bay leaves**
2 medium onions, chopped	**3 cups fish stock**
	salt and pepper
3 celery stalks, chopped	**cornstarch**
¼ cup cooking oil	

Boil fillets for 6 minutes; cool and cut into chunks. In large skillet, saute green peppers, onions and celery in cooking oil. Add tomatoes and bay leaves and cook until vegetables are tender. Add fish stock and trout chunks. Simmer for 5 minutes. Season fish with salt and pepper. Thicken with cornstarch. Serve over rice.

Thomas Largent
Beaverton, Michigan

Campfire Lake Trout

Serves: varies
Prep Time: 45 minutes

1 whole lake trout
salt and pepper to taste
butter to taste
plain yogurt
garlic (optional)
onions (optional)
lemons or limes, sliced

Fillet trout if desired. Season trout with salt and pepper. Add butter and put yogurt in cavity of fish. Put garlic, onions, lemon or lime slices on outside of fish. Wrap fish in aluminum foil. Place fish on coals (not fire) for approximately 30 minutes.

Jerry Gray
Jackson, Wyoming

Tasty Grilled Trout

Serves: 2
Prep Time: 20-25 minutes

2 **1-lb. trout fillets**	1 **T. garlic powder**
cooking oil	½ **T. salt**
1 **small onion, finely**	2 **bacon strips**
chopped	2 **Swiss cheese slices**
1 **T. lemon pepper**	2 **T. margarine**

Preheat grill on medium setting. Fold edges of aluminum foil piece to retain juices. Oil foil to prevent sticking. Place fillets on foil, covering with onion. Sprinkle salt, garlic, and lemon pepper evenly on each fillet and place bacon strip and cheese slice on top of each. Dot with margarine. Put aluminum foil on grill. Grill fillets for 15-20 minutes with lid closed.

Ronald Musgrave
Darby, Montana

Steelhead Supreme

Serves: 8
Prep Time: 30 minutes

1 **6-lb. steelhead**	4 **T. lemon juice**
4 **T. teriyaki sauce**	**garlic salt**
5 **garlic cloves, smashed**	**lemon pepper**
and chopped	

Preheat grill to medium heat. Fillet steelhead leaving skin on. Discard backbone. Combine ingredients to make marinade. Marinate fish for 30 minutes. Place fish on hot grill skin-side down and cool for 15 minutes. Turn pieces twice and baste; season lightly.

Cory West
Yuba City, California

Eddy's Stuffed Trout

Serves: 4
Prep Time: 30 minutes

3-5 lbs. fresh trout	**2 T. fresh parsley**
24 grapes (seeded)	**¼ cup dry white wine**
2 cups seasoned bread crumbs	**salt and pepper to taste**
½ lb. fresh mushrooms	**2 T. lemon juice**
1 large onion, finely chopped	

Clean trout and dry cavity with paper towel. Combine grapes, bread crumbs, mushrooms, onion and parsley in large mixing bowl. Moisten mixture with wine. Season fillets with salt and pepper and wipe cove with lemon juice. Stuff each trout with mixture and bake at 375 degrees for 45 minutes or until fish flakes easily.

Edward Phillips
Troy, New York

Microwaved Trout And Mushrooms

Serves: 3-4
Prep Time: 15 minutes

1 lb. fresh trout	**½ cup sliced mushrooms**
2 T. butter or margarine	**1 tomato, peeled and cubed**
½ tsp. lemon juice	**½ tsp. salt**
2 T. white wine	
2 green onions, thinly sliced	

Arrange trout in 12x7x2-inch microwavable baking dish. Dot with butter. Combine lemon juice with wine and drizzle over fillets. Sprinkle remaining ingredients over fish. Cover with plastic wrap. Cook on maximum power for 5 minutes. Let stand (covered) for 5 minutes before serving.

Gordon Krise
Harpursville, New York

Beer Steamed Lake Trout

Serves: 4-6
Prep Time: 30-40 minutes

2 **trout fillets (with skin)**	**butter**
2 **large onions, sliced in rings**	**garlic salt to taste**
lemon pepper salt	½ **can beer**

Lay onions on bed of aluminum foil. Place trout on onions skin-side down and season with lemon pepper salt. Add several pats of butter and garlic salt. Fold foil and seal at one end. Keep skin-side next to onion. Don't roll fillets. Open end of foil and pour in beer; seal. Place on gas grill or charcoal grill. Cook until fish flakes. Skin will remove easily.

Nelson Wertman
Romulus, New York

Baked Lake Michigan Trout

Serves: 4-8
Prep Time: 1 hour, 15 minutes

2-4 **lbs. trout fillets**	½ **tsp. dry mustard**
salt to taste	¼ **tsp. pepper**
¾ **cup mayonnaise**	¼ **tsp. parsley**
3 **T. lemon juice**	¼ **tsp. marjoram**
1 **tsp. onion powder**	¼ **tsp. sweet basil**

Lightly season fillets with salt and lay them in baking dish. Combine mayonnaise and seasonings; spread mixture over fish. Bake in preheated oven (2 lbs. fish at 400 degrees for 25-30 minutes; 3-4 lbs. fish at 375 degrees for 40-50 minutes). Fish is done when lightly brown.

William Rottler
Fountain, Michigan

Gourmet Trout Bake

Serves: 4
Prep Time: 30 minutes

4 lbs. trout fillets
salt and pepper to taste
½ lb. sliced mushrooms
2 T. butter

1 cup heavy cream
½ cup croutons
1 T. parsley, minced

Preheat oven to 400 degrees. Rub trout with salt and pepper. Arrange fillets in single layer in shallow baking dish. Saute mushrooms in butter for 3-5 minutes; remove from heat. Stir in cream and pour over trout. Cover loosely with aluminum foil and bake for 15-20 minutes or until trout flakes easily. Scatter croutons and parsley on top and serve.

Teresa Brown
Evansville, Wyoming

Trout In Foil

Serves: 6
Prep Time: 1 hour

trout fillets
1 onion, sliced
2 carrots, sliced
1 can peas
1 small can stewed tomatoes

2 potatoes, sliced
salt and pepper
butter
lemon juice

Cut fillets into serving-sized pieces. Place fillets on large piece of doubled aluminum foil. Cover fillets with vegetables. Season with salt and pepper. Add a little butter and drizzle with lemon juice. Fold both ends of foil together and upward. Cook on grill for about 40 minutes.

Thomas Largent
Beaverton, Michigan

Grilled Trout With Crab Stuffing

Serves: 3
Prep Time: 1 hour

3 **1-lb. trout, dressed with heads on**	2 **T. fresh parsley, chopped**
1 **egg**	½ **tsp. salt**
8 **oz. crabmeat, cleaned**	½ **tsp. pepper**
1 **cup seasoned bread crumbs**	2 **sticks butter**

Beat egg in mixing bowl. Add crabmeat, bread crumbs, parsley, salt and pepper; mix together thoroughly. Add more crumbs if you like. Melt butter and add 2 T. to mixture. Set the rest aside. Take stuffing and pack inside body cavity of trout. Put trout in fish-holding grill and place on outdoor grill. Use remaining melted butter to brush on trout while turning and cooking.

Michael Lozak
Parlin, New Jersey

Trout Amandine

Serves: 2
Prep Time: 30 minutes

4 **trout fillets**	1 **cup butter**
1 **cup milk**	½ **cup almonds, chopped**
1 **tsp. salt**	**lemon slices**
⅛ **tsp. pepper**	**parsley**
½ **cup flour**	

Dip fillets in milk. Then season with salt and pepper. Roll fillets in flour. In skillet, melt ¼ cup butter and brown fillets on both sides. Remove fish from skillet and add remaining butter. Saute almonds until golden. Serve over cooked fillets. Garnish with lemon slices and parsley.

Edward Phillips
Troy, New Jersey

Jim's Baked Trout

Serves: 2-4
Prep Time: 1 hour

2-4 medium trout	**garlic powder to taste**
½ stick butter	**⅓ cup parsley**
1 onion, chopped	**4 bacon strips**
seasoning salt to taste	

Line pan with aluminum foil. Place fish in pan. Stuff each trout cavity with a pat of butter and equal amounts of onion. Then sprinkle inside of cavity with seasoning salt and garlic powder; top with parsley. Wrap bacon slice around each trout's middle and fasten with toothpick. Sprinkle seasoning salt and garlic powder on top of trout. Cover with foil and bake at 325 degrees for 45 minutes.

James Uncapher
Johnstown, Pennsylvania

Ron's Trout Amandine

Serves: 4
Prep Time: 30 minutes

8 trout fillets	**½ cup slivered almonds**
½ cup flour	**3 T. dry white wine**
salt and pepper to taste	**6 parsley sprigs**
1 cup milk	**12 lemon wedges**
⅓ cup butter	

Season flour with salt and pepper. Dip fillets in milk and dredge in flour mixture. In skillet, brown fish on both sides in butter. Arrange fish on serving platter and keep warm. Saute almonds in butter and wine; pour mixture over fish. Garnish with parsley and lemon wedges.

Ronald Goll
Brooklyn Park, Minnesota

Tuna Swiss Pie

Serves: 8
Prep Time: 1 hour

13 oz. tuna
1 unbaked 9-inch pastry shell
1 cup Swiss cheese, shredded

½ cup green onion, sliced
3 eggs
1 cup mayonnaise
½ cup milk

Pierce pastry thoroughly with fork. Bake in oven at 375 degrees for 10 minutes; remove. In large bowl, combine next three ingredients; spoon into pastry shell. Stir remaining ingredients together and slowly pour over tuna mixture. Bake for 50 minutes or until knife comes out clean when inserted in center.

Eric Shields
Fort Wayne, Indiana

Tuna Surprise

Serves: 6
Prep Time: 10 minutes

20 oz. tuna
1 can cream of mushroom soup, condensed
½ cup milk
8 oz. cheddar cheese
1 tsp. yellow mustard
1 pkg. frozen peas

Heat soup and milk in saucepan until smooth, then add cheese. When cheese melts, add mustard and tuna. Cook peas in separate pan for 6-7 minutes, then add to mixture. Serve over hot biscuits or toast.

Steven Swartz
Clearbrook, Virginia

Carl's Supreme Tuna Surprise

Serves: 4
Prep Time: 30 minutes

- **36 oz. tuna**
- **12 oz. egg noodles**
- **1 16-oz. can carrots**
- **1 16-oz. can peas**
- **½ tsp. paprika**
- **1 cup onion, chopped**
- **½ tsp. mustard powder**
- **1 cup cheddar cheese**
- **1 green pepper**
- **5 fresh ginger slices (thin)**
- **lemon juice**
- **1 tsp. brandy extract**
- **1 tsp. chives**
- **parsley**
- **½ tsp. cajun powder**
- **bread crumbs**
- **3 T. flour**

Boil noodles in 4-qt. pan of slightly salted water. In large bowl mix all ingredients except parsley and bread crumbs. Add drained noodles. Preheat oven to 325 degrees. Pour noodle mixture into casserole dish or pan. Top with bread crumbs and parsley. Bake for 30 minutes.

Charles Hoffman
Albany, New York

Walleye Fish Sticks

Serves: 4
Prep Time: 35 minutes

1½ **walleye fillets, cut into**
1-inch strips
3 **1-oz. French bread**
slices, cubed
½ **tsp. pepper**
3 **T. mayonnaise**
1 **tsp. lemon juice**
2 **tsp. water**
½ **tsp. lemon rind, grated**

Put bread cubes and pepper into food processor for 30 seconds, until crumbs are fine. Sprinkle crumbs in an ungreased baking sheet and bake at 350 degrees for 10 minutes or until browned. Put in bowl and set aside. Combine mayonnaise, lemon juice, water and rind in separate bowl. Stir well. Dip fish strips in mixture of mayonnaise, then in bread crumbs. Place on baking sheet coated with cooking spray. Bake at 400 degrees for 25 minutes, or until outside is crispy.

James Saver Jr.
Larsen, Wisconsin

Broiled Walleye Fillets

Serves: 4
Prep Time: 10-15 minutes

2-4 **lbs. walleye fillets**
brown sugar to taste
ground pepper

Sprinkle brown sugar and pepper on fillets. Broil fish in oven or on barbecue grill until flaky (about 3-6 minutes). Serve with lemon and tartar sauce.

Steve Paleck
Rapid City, South Dakota

Walleye With Almonds

Serves: 2
Prep Time: 30 minutes

- **2 walleye fillets**
- **1 egg**
- **¼ cup milk**
- **¼ cup slivered almonds**
- **½ cup flour**
- **salt and pepper**
- **olive oil**
- **green onions, finely chopped**

Combine egg and milk. Soak fillets in egg mixture, then dredge in almond and flour. Saute fillets in olive oil over medium heat until crust is medium brown. Turn fillets, adding more almonds to top. Continue cooking fish until crust is medium brown. (Do not overcook.) Season with salt and pepper and green onions to taste. Serve with wild rice and fresh fruit.

Foster William Chapman III
Minnetonka, Minnesota

Quick Baked Walleye Fillets

Serves: 4-6
Prep Time: 30 minutes

- **2 lbs. walleye fillets**
- **flour or pancake mix**
- **salt and pepper to taste**
- **garlic powder to taste**

Preheat oven to 500 degrees. Season fillets with salt, pepper and garlic powder. Dip fillets in flour and place in lightly greased 9x13-inch baking pan. Bake uncovered for 10-15 minutes or until fish flakes easily with fork.

Teresa Brown
Evansville, Wyoming

Walleye Italiano

Serves: 4-6
Prep Time: 30 minutes

1 **5-lb. walleye, cleaned**
⅔ **cup onion, finely chopped**
⅔ **cup carrot, finely chopped**
⅔ **cup celery, finely chopped**
 several parsley sprigs
 thyme sprig

1 **bay leaf**
2 **garlic cloves, crushed**
 salt and pepper to taste
1½ **cups red wine**
½ **cup water**
3 **T. butter**
3 **T. flour**
 juice of 1 lemon

Grease Dutch oven. Add all vegetables, herbs, salt, pepper, wine and water. Bring to a boil over medium heat. Place fish on bed of vegetables and simmer for 18 minutes. While fish is cooking, melt butter and flour. Stir until thick. Add lemon juice. Pour over fish and serve.

Michael Bailey
Nineveh, Indiana

Barbecued Walleye Fillets

Serves: 4
Prep Time: 25 minutes

2 **lbs. walleye fillets**
½ **cup onion, minced**
½ **cup butter**
4 **tsp. Worcestershire sauce**

4 **tsp. catsup**
2 **tsp. vinegar**

In skillet, saute onion in butter until tender. Add Worcestershire sauce, catsup and vinegar; stir to blend. Cut fillets and place in sauce. Cover and simmer for 10 minutes. Turn fillets and simmer for 10-15 minutes or until fish flakes easily when tested with fork.

John Craig
Shelocta, Pennsylvania

Steamed Walleye In Microwave

Serves: 4
Prep Time: 15 minutes

1 **lb. walleye, skinned**	1 **large onion, chopped**
¼ **cup melted butter**	1 **green pepper, chopped**
¼ **cup lemon juice**	1 **large tomato, chopped**
2 **tsp. garlic powder**	**salt and pepper to taste**
1 **tsp. sweet basil**	2 **tsp. water**

Butter each side of walleye. Put lemon juice, garlic powder, basil and onion on top of fillets. Then place green pepper and tomato on top. Season with salt and pepper. Place on microwave pan and add water. Cover with plastic wrap. Cook on high for 15 minutes.

Richard Scott
Conneaut, Ohio

Broiled Walleye

Serves: varies
Prep Time: 15 minutes

2 **walleye fillets per**
person
garlic powder or salt
pepper
paprika
parsley
onion pieces
melted butter

Place fish in baking dish and sprinkle with seasonings and onion. Broil for 5 minutes. Drizzle with melted butter. Broil 1 minute. Turn fish and broil 5 minutes more. Drizzle with butter and broil 1 minute again. Serve with pan drippings.

Ron Pasch
Freeport, Illinois

Beer Batter Fillets

Serves: 4-6
Prep Time: 5 minutes

8 medium walleye fillets	**¾ tsp. salt**
2 egg whites	**2 egg yolks**
1 cup flour	**1 cup beer**
½ tsp. baking soda	**½ cup shortening**

Whip egg whites. Combine flour, soda, salt, egg yolks and beer. (Mixture can be thinned to taste by adding more beer or thickened by adding more flour.) Fold in egg whites. Dip fish fillets in batter and fry in shortening until golden brown.

James Sontag
Pocatello, Idaho

Baked Fillet Of Walleye

Serves: 4
Prep Time: 35 minutes

2-4 lbs. walleye fillets
salt and pepper to taste
butter, melted
1 cup celery soup,
condensed
¼ cup cream
¼ cup sherry
Parmesan cheese,
grated

Season fillets with salt and pepper, then dip in melted butter. Place fillets in shallow baking pan. Mix celery soup with cream and sherry. Cover fillets with this mixture and sprinkle grated Parmesan cheese over fillets. Bake for 30 minutes at 350 degrees.

Tom Ruhl
Princeton, Wisconsin

Grilled Poached Walleye

Serves: 6
Prep Time: 20 minutes

3-4 lbs. walleye fillets
2 tsp. salt
1 tsp. black pepper
4 T. lemon juice
4-5 T. water
1 medium onion, chopped
1 tsp. ground dried
parsley
3 T. butter or margarine

Rub salt and pepper into fish and drizzle with lemon juice. Sprinkle onion and parsley over fish and add water. Wrap fish up in aluminum foil with butter and place on barbecue coals or rack. Cook for 20 minutes, turning every 5 minutes.

Randy Sautter
Crookston, Minnesota

Fish Creole

Serves: 4
Prep Time: 30 minutes

4 walleye fillets
1 green pepper, chopped
1 onion, chopped
1 garlic clove, chopped
¼ cup celery, chopped
¼ cup butter
2 cups catsup
1 cup water

Saute green pepper, onion, garlic and celery in butter until tender. Add catsup and water. Bring to a boil. While creole is cooking, bake fillets at 350 degrees, or fry in butter for 15 minutes. Pour creole over fillets and bake or fry for another 10 minutes.

Mark Nieman
Hawarden, Iowa

Grilled Weakfish With Vegetables

Serves: 4
Prep Time: 45 minutes

- **6 weakfish fillets**
- **1 cup Italian dressing**
- **1 T. Old Bay seasoning**
  salt and pepper
- **1 tomato, sliced**
- **1 scallion, sliced**
- **1 green or red pepper,**
  sliced
- **½ stick butter**
- **⅓ cup lemon juice**

Soak fish in Italian dressing for 15 minutes. Take 3 pieces of aluminum foil and place 2 fillets on each piece. Sprinkle Old Bay seasoning, salt and pepper and vegetables over fish. Place dollop of butter on each fillet and drizzle with lemon juice. Fold foil securely and place on grill with low setting. Cook for 15-20 minutes or until fish is flaky. Garnish with toasted garlic bread.

Lisa Sinclair
Salem, New Jersey

Garlic Yellowtail

Serves: 4
Prep Time: 25 minutes

4 large yellowtail fillets
2 eggs
 bread crumbs
 olive oil
2 garlic cloves, chopped

Dip fillets in beaten eggs and roll in bread crumbs. Pour olive oil into frying pan and add garlic cloves. Add fish when oil is hot. Fry both sides and serve.

Oswaldo Tapanes
Miami, Florida

Connecticut Chowder

Serves: 4
Prep Time: 25 minutes

1 **large fish, skinned and boned**	2 **T. parsley, minced**
½ **tsp. lemon pepper**	5-6 **potatoes, diced**
1-2 **tsp. seasoned salt**	1½ **cups carrots, peeled and thickly shredded**
6-8 **bacon slices, diced**	2 **qts. whole milk**
1 **large onion, diced**	1 **cup canned corn, drained (optional)**
flour	

Cut fish into bite-sized pieces. Simmer fish pieces with spices for 15-20 minutes. (Do not add too much water, just enough to cover.) Meanwhile saute bacon and onion until bacon is crisp and onion is tender. Drain grease and toss bacon and onion with flour and parsley. To chowder, add bacon, onion and potatoes. Make sure potatoes are covered with liquid. (Add more if needed.) Add carrots and simmer until potatoes are tender and liquid is reduced. Add milk and more seasonings if needed, heating thoroughly. (Do not boil.) Add butter and sprinkle with more parsley. Add canned corn at this time.

Walter Squier
Portland, Connecticut

Barbecued Fish Fillets

Serves: varies
Prep Time: 15 minutes

fish fillets	**lemon juice**
bacon slices	**butter**
onion, sliced	

Roll fillet around onion slice. Next, wrap fillet in bacon slice, using toothpicks to fasten. Barbecue on low flame, basting with lemon juice and butter.

Gerald Timmerman
Bishop, California

Warm Fish Salad With Blue Cheese

Serves: 4
Prep Time: 40 minutes

½ **lb. fish fillets**
fresh spinach leaves
1 **cup fresh mushrooms**
½ **cup celery, thinly sliced**
2 **small tomatoes, seeded**
¼ **cup green pepper**
3 **T. olive or cooking oil**
¼ **cup red wine vinegar**
½ **cup red onion, sliced**

1 **T. Worcestershire sauce**
½ **tsp. dried parsley**
½ **tsp. dried basil**
½ **tsp. dried oregano**
¼ **tsp. salt**
¼ **tsp. pepper**
⅔ **cup canned garbanzo beans, drained**
3 **T. blue cheese**

Line 4 dinner plates with spinach leaves; set aside. Combine sliced mushrooms, celery, chopped tomatoes and chopped green peppers in large bowl. In skillet, heat 2 T. oil and 2 T. vinegar. Add onion and cook (covered) for 2 minutes. Remove onion with slotted spoon, add to vegetable mixture. To skillet add remaining vinegar and oil, Worcestershire sauce, parsley, basil, oregano, salt and pepper. Add fish strips and cook until done. Add beans and heat thoroughly. Toss fish mixture with vegetables. Divide mixture among plates. Sprinkle blue cheese on each.

Dennis Breiner
Wichita, Kansas

Beer Batter Fish

Serves: 4
Prep Time: 15 minutes

fish fillets
2 **eggs, beaten**
1 **cup flour**

1 **tsp. baking powder**
1 **tsp. salt**
1 **cup beer**

Beat all ingredients together. Dredge fish in flour. Dip fish into batter and fry in deep fat at 375 degrees until brown.

Jeffrey Chmiel
Buffalo, New York

Courtbouillon

Serves: 6-8
Prep Time: 2 hours

3 lbs. fillets, broiled
1 cup flour
1 cup shortening
butter
lemon juice
paprika
6 cups tomato sauce
1 can stewed whole
tomatoes
4 qts. water

1½ T. parsley, chopped
¾ cup green onions,
chopped
2 tsp. salt
3 tsp. red pepper
2½ tsp. garlic salt
2 T. Worcestershire sauce
2½ tsp. black pepper
3 tsp. paprika
2 bay leaves

To make roux: Brown flour in shortening until deep brown, being careful not to burn. Broil fish with butter, lemon juice and paprika. Simmer all ingredients (except fillets and bay leaves) for 30 minutes. Add broiled fish to pot and cover. Simmer for 30 minutes, stirring gently to keep from sticking and burning. Turn off heat and add bay leaves. Let cool for 15 minutes. Serve over cooked rice and with lots of cold liquids!

Al Wilson
Port Neches, Texas

Fish Cakes

Serves: 4
Prep Time: 20 minutes

1½ cups fish, boned
1½ cups bread crumbs
1 egg
1 tsp. parsley

¼ tsp. salt
⅛ tsp. pepper
½ cup oil

Combine fish, bread crumbs, egg, parsley, salt and pepper. Mix well and shape into patties. Heat oil and fry for 2-3 minutes on each side or until brown.

Steven Swartz
Clearbrook, Virginia

Fish And Vegetable Bake

Serves: varies
Prep Time: 15 minutes

fish fillets
cooking oil
salt and pepper
carrots, sliced
onions, sliced
green peppers, sliced

celery, sliced
tomatoes, sliced
butter or margarine
Parmesan cheese,
grated

Preheat oven to 350 degrees. Each fillet will have its own aluminum foil sheet. Cut each foil sheet 4 inches longer than its fillet. Rub cooking oil on foil and leave at least 2-inch margin on all sides. Season fillets with salt and pepper to taste. Place fillets on center of foil. Cover fillets with sliced vegetables. Lightly season with salt and pepper again. Dot fillets with butter and sprinkle cheese over fillets. Fold foil lengthwise, leaving some air space inside. Then, fold foil tightly on each end of fillet. Place foil packs on cookie sheet and bake for 15 minutes or more, depending on thickness of fillets.

Elmer Jensen
Eagle River, Wisconsin

Fish In Foil Over Fire

Serves: 4
Prep Time: 30 minutes

4 1-lb. fish fillets
2 garlic cloves
1 large onion

salt and pepper to taste
¼ cup beer

Place fish in aluminum foil with tails intact. Finely chop garlic and onion. Sprinkle garlic, onion and salt and pepper over fish. Add beer. Make sure foil is wrapped tightly. Cook over campfire on open flame until done, turning frequently.

Charles Stewart
Jeannette, Pennsylvania

Quick Swiss Fish Rolls

Serves: 4
Prep Time: 10 minutes

1 **lb. fish fillets, thawed**
6 **oz. Swiss cheese**
¾ **cup milk**
¼ **T. salt**
1 **T. cornstarch**
¼ **cup white wine or sherry**
2 **T. butter**

½ **T. Worcestershire sauce**
1 **T. dried parsley (optional)**
Tabasco sauce (optional)
¼ **cup ripe olives, chopped (optional)**

Rinse fillets and pat dry on paper towels. Cut fillets into 5-inch strips. Slice cheese into ¼x3-inch sticks. Use 1 cheese stick for each roll. Heat salt with milk over low heat in skillet. Roll each fillet around cheese stick and place in milk. Cover and simmer for 5 minutes, turning carefully. Cook for 5 more minutes until fish is opaque and cheese is melted. Remove fish and keep warm. Add cornstarch, butter and Worcestershire sauce. Tabasco sauce, parsley and olives can be added to milk, if desired. Stir until thickened and pour over fish rolls.

Harold Baker
Colorado Springs, Colorado

Grilled Fillets

Serves: 4
Prep Time: 30 minutes

2 **lbs. fish fillets**
1 **tsp. barbecue seasoning**
1 **tsp. all seasoning**

1 **tsp. black pepper**
1 **stick butter**
1 **tsp. bacon drippings**

Combine seasonings, butter and drippings. Melt in microwave and stir. Place fish on grill over medium heat. Use fish basket if available. Spoon or brush season mix over fish. Keep fish moist. Cook to desired tenderness.

Patricia Jones
South Daytona, Florida

Red Wine Fish

Serves: 1-2
Prep Time: 30 minutes

fish fillets	2 **lbs. tomatoes, crushed**
olive oil	2 **large tomatoes**
10 **garlic cloves, chopped**	1 **can anchovies**
2 **large onions, chopped**	4 **oz. black olives**
1 **T. thyme**	2 **oz. capers**
3 **T. basil**	½ **cup parsley**
1 **pt. red wine**	

Heat olive oil for 30 seconds in large pot. Add garlic and onions; stir. Lower heat to medium. Cook onions until transparent, but not brown. Add thyme and basil; stir and cook for 2 minutes. Add 2 cups red wine and crushed tomatoes. Bring to a boil. Then simmer uncovered for 10 minutes. Add fresh tomatoes, anchovies, black olives and capers. Simmer on low heat for 5 minutes. Remove from heat, seasoning with salt and pepper again. Arrange fillets so they do not touch. Ladle sauce over fillets. Bake uncovered at 400 degrees for 15 minutes. Serve with parsley.

Shawn Swenson
Torrance, California

Baked Fillets

Serves: 4
Prep Time: 20 minutes

4 **fish fillets**
¼ **cup margarine**
1 **chicken bouillon cube**
pepper

Melt margarine and chicken bouillon in glass baking dish. Add fillets, turning to coat both sides. Bake at 500 degrees for 10-12 minutes, turning once. Pepper can be added before or after.

Barb Conley
Louisville, Nebraska

Fish And Asparagus Bundles

Serves: 4
Prep Time: 30 minutes or less

4 fish fillets	**½ cup mushrooms, sliced**
¾ lb. fresh asparagus (or 10 oz. frozen)	**2 tomatoes, peeled and chopped**
2 T. olive oil	**⅓ cup dry white wine**
½ cup celery and tops, sliced	**1 tsp. basil**
½ cup onion, chopped	**1 T. butter**
1 garlic clove, minced	**salt to taste**

Cut asparagus into 6-inch lengths and cook in small amount of boiling salted water for 8-10 minutes or until almost tender; drain. In olive oil, saute celery, onion, garlic and mushrooms for 3-5 minutes. Add tomatoes, wine and basil. Simmer while preparing fillets. Dab fillets with butter; season with a little salt. Place asparagus across fillets; roll up fillets and fasten with toothpicks. Place fish rolls seam-side down in skillet. Cover tightly; simmer for 7-8 minutes or until fish flakes easily.

Traci Nagy
Cuyahoga Falls, Ohio

Baked Fish

Serves: 6
Prep Time: 15 minutes

2 lbs. fish, boned	**⅓ cup butter, melted**
¼ tsp. salt	**3 T. soy sauce**
⅛ tsp. pepper	**3 T. lemon juice**
⅛ tsp. onion powder	

Heat oven to 350 degrees. Place fish in 13x9-inch pan. Sprinkle salt, pepper, garlic and onion powder on fish. Combine melted butter, soy sauce and lemon juice. Pour over fish. Bake for 15 minutes, basting often.

Warren Miller
Princeton, Minnesota

Baked Fish Fillets

Serves: 4-6
Prep Time: 1 hour

2-3 **lbs. fillets, skinned**	1 **cup water**
1½ **T. melted butter**	**salt and pepper to taste**
1 **T. flour**	½ **T. lemon juice**
1 **medium onion, minced**	½ **cup bread crumbs**
½ **bay leaf**	
1 **cup chicken stock or 1**	
chicken bouillon cube	

Cut fillets into serving-sized pieces and place on greased baking dish. In saucepan, combine melted butter, flour and onion, blending thoroughly. Add bay leaf. Dissolve chicken stock in water and add to saucepan. Simmer for 15 minutes, stirring until mixture has thickened. Remove bay leaf. Season with salt and pepper and lemon juice. Pour mixture over fish. Sprinkle bread crumbs on top and bake at 425 degrees for about 20 minutes. If desired, sprinkle Parmesan cheese over bread crumbs.

Robert Hill Jr.
Tullahoma, Tennessee

Broiled Fish Fillets

Serves: 6
Prep Time: 15 minutes

6 **fish fillets**	¼ **stick margarine, melted**
1 **tsp. Worcestershire**	½ **cup white wine**
sauce	1 **tsp. fresh basil, chopped**
1 **garlic clove, crushed**	

Combine Worcestershire sauce, garlic, margarine and wine. Mix thoroughly, then brush mixture over fillets. Broil for 3-4 minutes. Turn fillets over and brush with mixture again. Broil another 4-6 minutes. Sprinkle basil over top and serve.

Barb Conley
Louisville, Nebraska

Dan's Baked Fish Fillets

Serves: 6
Prep Time: 20-30 minutes

2 lbs. fish fillets
2 T. lemon juice
¾ tsp. salt
¼ cup flour
½ cup butter or
margarine, melted

1 cup cornflakes or
crackers, finely crushed
tartar sauce
capers, drained
dill or parsley sprigs

Rinse fish under cold water and drain on paper towels. Slice fish into 6 portions, cutting tail portions larger. Fold end of tail under for even cooking. Combine next 4 ingredients in shallow pan until smooth. Put cornflake or cracker crumbs into another shallow pan. Dip fish in flour-butter mixture, then dip into dry coating. Bake at 400 degrees for about 20 minutes or until fish is well browned and flakes easily. Garnish with tartar sauce, capers and fresh dill or parsley sprigs.

Danny Hummel
Essex, Iowa

Cheese Fish Bake

Serves: 2
Prep Time: 30-40 minutes

1 lb. fish fillets
pepper to taste
1 cup mushroom soup,
condensed

¾ cup cheddar cheese,
shredded
paprika

Put fillets in well-greased casserole dish and sprinkle with pepper. Pour soup over fish and cover with cheddar cheese. Top with paprika. Bake at 375 degrees for 40 minutes or until browned.

Virgil Jensen
Battle Lake, Minnesota

Fish Roll-Ups

Serves: 4
Prep Time: 20 minutes

8 fillets (thin)
½ cup horseradish sauce (mild)
2 T. yellow mustard
1 T. fresh basil, chopped
1 egg yolk, beaten

8 bacon slices
8 green onions, cut to width of fillets
your favorite batter (thin)
vegetable oil

Mix horseradish sauce, mustard, sweet basil and egg yolk until creamy. Spread mixture in even layers in complete inside portions of fillets. Lay bacon slices lengthwise on each fillet. Lay green onions across large end of each fillet. Fold large end over onion and continue to roll up entire fillet. Secure with 2-3 toothpicks. Dip fillets in your favorite batter (very thin) to coat. Deep-fry fillets in vegetable oil until done. Make sure to use thin fillets or inside will not get done. These can also be made in oven: Bake for 30 minutes at 350 degrees.

Charlie Ladd
Bowling Green, Ohio

Fish Chowder

Serves: 4
Prep Time: 30-45 minutes

2 lbs. fish fillets
6 medium potatoes, diced
4 medium onions, diced
¼ stick butter

fresh or canned milk to taste
salt and pepper

Place potatoes and onions in large pan, cover with water and boil until done. Add fish fillets, cooking until tender. Add butter and milk. Heat, but do not boil. Season with salt and pepper to taste. For thicker chowder, use less water and milk or add more fish.

John Craig
Shelocta, Pennsylvania

Fresh Catch Parmesan

Serves: 4
Prep Time: 30 minutes

1 **lb. fish fillets**	½ **cup oil**
½ **cup flour**	2 **cups spaghetti sauce**
½ **cup seasoned bread crumbs**	1 **cup mozzarella cheese, shredded**
salt and pepper to taste	¼ **cup Parmesan cheese, grated**
1 **egg**	

In pie plate, combine flour and bread crumbs, seasoning with salt and pepper. Dip each fillet in crumb mixture, then in well beaten egg, returning to flour mixture again. Make sure fillets are well coated. Place each fillet in hot oil until each side is browned. Then drain on paper towel. Spread spaghetti sauce in bottom of shallow baking dish. Lay fish in dish, covering with remaining sauce. Cover each piece with mozzarella and then Parmesan cheese. Bake at 325 degrees for about 20 minutes. Serve with spaghetti, salad and hot bread.

Dennis Breiner
Wichita, Kansas

Delicious Fish Patties

Serves: 4
Prep Time: 15-20 minutes

1 **cup fish, flaked and cooked**	**pepper to taste**
1 **egg**	1 **cup mashed potatoes (cold)**
1 **tsp. minced onion**	2 **T. flour**
1 **tsp. lemon juice**	**shortening or cooking oil**
1 **tsp. salt**	

Beat egg and combine with fish, onion, lemon juice, seasonings and potatoes. Form into patties, coating with flour to help shape. Fry in hot shortening or oil.

Matthew Olexa
Bloomsburg, Pennsylvania

Meal-In-One Seafood Platter

Serves: 6
Prep Time: 20 minutes

2 lbs. fish fillets
½ cup lemon juice
3 T. butter
2 T. onion, grated
2 T. brown sugar, firmly packed
1 tsp. dry mustard

½ tsp. salt
¼ tsp. pepper
paprika
frozen carrot nuggets, cooked
frozen asparagus spears, cooked

Put fillets in single layer in shallow baking pan. In saucepan, mix lemon juice, butter, onion, brown sugar, dry mustard, salt and pepper. Heat and stir until blended. Pour sauce over fish. Broil fish 3-4 inches from heat source for 10-15 minutes or until fish flakes easily. While broiling, baste fillets 2-3 times with lemon juice mixture. Transfer fillets to warm platter. Sprinkle with paprika. Arrange hot carrots and asparagus spears on platter and serve.

Stan Volk
Crestline, Ohio

Grilled Fish

Serves: 4
Prep Time: 15-20 minutes

4 fish fillets
salt to taste (optional)
cayenne pepper to taste
black pepper to taste

2 lemons, thinly sliced
1 small onion, thinly sliced

Place fillets in large piece of aluminum foil. Season fillets with salt, cayenne pepper and pepper. Cover each fillet with lemon and onion slices, then seal foil tightly. Put foil packet on grill and cook for 15-20 minutes or until fish flakes.

Leslie Gaines
Mount Vernon, Texas

Poached Fillets In Cheese Sauce

Serves: 2-3
Prep Time: 20-30 minutes

1 **lb. fish fillets**	¼ **tsp. Worcestershire**
1 **cup milk**	**sauce or soy sauce**
3 **T. dry sherry or**	3 **drops hot sauce**
chicken broth	4 **oz. sharp cheddar**
½ **tsp. salt**	**cheese**
¼ **tsp. pepper**	**parsley, chopped**
2 **T. flour**	

Put ¾ cup milk in flat pan. Add sherry or broth, salt and pepper. Stir to blend and simmer. Add fillets and gently poach until done. Remove fillets to warm serving plate. Cover with another plate to keep warm. Blend flour and remaining milk; add to simmering liquid. Blend in with whisk. Add Worcestershire sauce and hot sauce. Sprinkle cheese over sauce, blending until melted. Pour sauce over fillets and garnish with parsley. Serve with sauteed mushrooms and broccoli or a green salad.

Walter Squier
Portland, Connecticut

Ma's Pickled Fish

Serves: 3-4
Prep Time: 15-30 minutes

2 **lbs. fish fillets**	1 **medium onion**
1 **cup sugar**	1 **T. mixed pickling spice**
1 **cup vinegar**	**salt and pepper to taste**
2 **cups water**	

When filleting fish, leave skin intact. Mix all other ingredients in pan and bring to a boil. Add raw fish. Continue boiling until fish is flaky. Remove all ingredients from pan and place in glass bowl. Let cool and serve.

Bob Trnka
Waseca, Minnesota

Pickled Fish

Serves: 3-4
Prep Time: 10 days

1 **qt. fresh whitefish fillets**	1 **cup white vinegar**
¾ **cup coarse pickling salt**	1 **medium white onion, sliced into rings**
2½ **cups white vinegar**	8-10 **whole cloves**
1 **cup sugar**	**bay leaves**

Cut fillets into bite-sized pieces. Prepare brine of ¾ cup salt and 1 cup white vinegar. Soak fish in brine for 4 days, stirring daily. After fourth day, rinse fish in cold water. Heat, but do not boil. Add sugar and 1 cup white vinegar. Layer fish, onion rings, cloves and bay leaves in fruit jars or plastic ice-cream containers. After vinegar-sugar mixture cools, add remaining wine and pour over fish. (Be sure to cover entire fish.) Let stand at least 1 week before eating.

William Trout
Des Moines, Iowa

Pancake-Battered Fish

Serves: 4-6
Prep Time: 15 minutes

2 **lbs. fish fillets**	¼ **tsp. salt**
cooking oil	¼ **tsp. pepper**
2 **cups pancake mix**	¼ **tsp. garlic or onion**
2 **cups milk**	**powder (optional)**

Cut fillets into serving-sized pieces. Heat oil until it ignites a match. (Use caution.) Place mix in large bowl. Stir in milk and seasonings. Dip fillets into batter; drain excess. Fry fillets until golden brown.

Dennis Hughes
Deer Lodge, Montana

Whitefish Soup

Serves: 4-6
Prep Time: 30 minutes

8 oz. fish, cubed	**2 cups heavy cream**
4 T. olive oil	**salt and pepper to taste**
½ cup onion, finely chopped	**2 pats butter**
2 T. flour	**¼ cup scallions, finely chopped**
½ cup clam juice	**½ cup potatoes, cubed and steamed**
½ cup white wine	

Heat olive oil for 30 seconds in saucepan. Add onion and cook for 2 minutes, stirring frequently. Add flour to onion mixture, mixing with whisk or spoon until oil absorbs flour. Add clam juice and wine, and beat mixture for about 1 minute. (Don't stop or you'll get lumps.) Cook for 2 minutes. Add cream and boil. Let soup boil again, cooking until fish is done. Season with salt and pepper. Add a pat of butter to each bowl. Serve with scallion and potatoes.

Michael Bailey
Nineveh, Indiana

Poached Fish

Serves: 5
Prep Time: 10 minutes

1⅞ lbs. fish fillets	**1¼ tsp. salt**
1¼ onion, chopped	**⅓ tsp. pepper**
5 lemon slices	**1¼ tsp. dill weed, chopped**
1¼ T. parsley, chopped	

In large skillet, combine all ingredients except fish in 1 inch of water and bring to a boil. Place fish in single layer in skillet. Cover and simmer until fish flakes easily, about 5 minutes.

Joseph Trojanowski
Fort Worth, Texas

Grilled Fish In Foil

Serves: 6
Prep Time: 45-60 minutes

2 **lbs. fish fillets**	2 **tsp. salt (optional)**
2 **green peppers, sliced**	2 **T. lemon juice**
2 **onions, sliced**	1 **tsp. paprika**
¼ **cup margarine, melted**	**dash of pepper**

Cut fillets into serving-sized portions. Cut 6 pieces of
heavy-duty aluminum foil, 12x12 inches each. Grease foil lightly.
Place a portion of fish, skin-side down, on foil. Top with green
peppers and onion. Combine remaining ingredients. Pour
sauce over fish. Bring foil up over fish and close all edges with
tight double folds. Place packages on grill about 5 inches from
moderately hot coals. Cook for 45 minutes or until fish flakes
easily when tested with fork.

Don Crowley Sr.
Milford, Massachusetts

Fillets Pan-Fried

Serves: 2-4
Prep Time: 30 minutes

2-4 **fish fillets**	**peanut oil**
2 **eggs, beaten**	**lemon pepper**
soda crackers, finely	**salt**
crushed	
dried onion rings,	
crushed	

Soak fillets in beaten eggs. In sealable plastic bag, add
crushed crackers, onion rings and fillets; shake until coated.
Panfry until golden brown in oil, adding lemon pepper and salt
to taste. Serve with lemon wedges.

Foster William Chapman III
Minnetonka, Minnesota

Baked Fish Steaks

Serves: 6
Prep Time: 1 hour

2 **lbs. fish steaks, fresh or frozen**
½ **cup French dressing**
2 **T. lemon juice**
¼ **tsp. salt (optional)**

1 **2.8-oz. can French-fried onions, crushed**
¼ **cup Parmesan cheese, grated**

Thaw steaks if frozen. Cut into serving-sized pieces. Place fish in shallow baking dish. Combine dressing, lemon juice and salt. Pour sauce over fish, marinating for 30 minutes, turning once. Remove fish from sauce and place in well-greased baking dish. In separate bowl, combine onions and cheese, mixing thoroughly. Sprinkle onion mix over fish. Bake at 350 degrees for 25-30 minutes, or until fish flakes easily.

Don Crowley Sr.
Milford, Massachusetts

Smoked Fillets

Serves: 4
Prep Time: 1 hour

3 **lbs. fish fillets**
1 **stick butter, melted**
½ **tsp. Tabasco sauce**
¼ **cup parsley, chopped**
   juice of 1 lemon
½ **tsp. Worcestershire sauce**

Cover tray with aluminum foil. Place fish on tray in single layer. Combine all other ingredients and pour over fish fillets. Place tray on grill in preheated smoker. Cover with top and cook for approximately 45 minutes or until done.

Al Wilson
Port Neches, Texas

Freshwater Whitefish

Serves: 4
Prep Time: 20 minutes

1½ **lbs. whitefish fillets, skinned**
½ **tsp. salt (optional)**
¼ **tsp. pepper**
4 **oz. instant mashed potato flakes**
½ **oz. dry garlic-style salad dressing mix**

1 **egg, beaten**
⅛ **cup butter, melted**
  dash of paprika
1 **T. lemon juice, freshly squeezed**

Cut fillets into four pieces. Season fish with salt and pepper. Combine potato flakes and salad dressing, mixing in bowl. Dip fillets into beaten egg, then dry mixture to coat. Place fillets on buttered baking dish and sprinkle with paprika. Bake at 500 degrees for 10 minutes or until done. Drizzle with lemon juice and serve.

Susan Cook
Holcomb, New York

Boiled Fish

Serves: varies
Prep Time: 20 minutes

fish, any kind
seafood seasoning
salt to taste
1 **medium onion, chopped**

¼ **cup lemon juice**
  lemon wedge
  parsley sprig
  melted butter

Combine fish, seafood seasoning, salt, onion and lemon juice. Boil until skin of fish lifts off, about 5-10 minutes (depending on size of fish). Serve fish whole (with or without head). Garnish with lemon wedge and parsley sprig. Place melted butter in side bowl for dipping.

Doc Smyk
Jacksonville, Florida

Savory Outdoor Baked Fish

Serves: 1 fish per person
Prep Time: 20-30 minutes

fish
butter or oil
salt and pepper to taste
lemon juice

tomato or pimiento to taste
lemon slices

Place cleaned, filleted fish on individual sheets of heavy-duty aluminum foil. Brush fillets with oil or melted butter. Sprinkle salt and pepper and lemon juice over fish. Top each fish with 1 tsp. chopped tomato or pimiento. Garnish with lemon slices. Bring foil up over fish and seal with a double fold (seal ends). Place on grate over medium-high fire and bake for 10 minutes per side for 1-1½-lb. fish; 15 minutes for 2- to 3-lb. fish; and 20 minutes for 4- to 5-lb. fish. Open foil and test with fork for easy flaking. Serve with juice from package.

Chad Bjorgaard
Viking, Minnesota

Broiled Fish Dijon

Serves: 4
Prep Time: 15-20 minutes

1½ **lbs. fish fillets**
 ½ **cup mayonnaise**
  3 **T. Parmesan cheese, grated**

2 **T. Dijon mustard**
  fresh ground pepper
  fresh parsley, chopped

Rinse fish and pat dry. Line cookie sheet or baking pan with aluminum foil. Combine mayonnaise, Parmesan cheese, mustard and pepper in bowl. Spread mixture over fish. Broil about 5 inches from heat source for 5-8 minutes or until fish flakes. Sprinkle parsley over fish and serve immediately with boiled potatoes and fresh green beans.

James Strunk
Philadelphia, Pennsylvania

Seafarer's Dinner

Serves: 4
Prep Time: 1 hour

1 **lb. fish fillets, thawed
  and drained**
2 **cups potatoes, sliced**
1 **cup carrot, cut into
  strips**
1 **medium onion, cut into
  strips**

½ **tsp. dill weed**
½ **tsp. salt**
⅛ **tsp. pepper**
¼ **cup butter**
¼ **cup Parmesan cheese,
  grated**
¼ **tsp. paprika**

Heat oven to 425 degrees. In 1½-qt. casserole dish, layer half of potatoes, carrots, onion and fish. Sprinkle half of dill weed, salt, pepper and butter over mixture. Then, repeat layering procedure. Cover and bake for 35-40 minutes. Remove cover and sprinkle cheese and paprika over top. Continue baking for 10 minutes or until vegetables are tender.

Dale Meyer
Kensett, Iowa

Easy Barbecue Fish

Serves: 2-4
Prep Time: 30 minutes

1½ **lbs. fish fillets**
 ¼ **cup butter or margarine**
 ½ **lemon**
   salt and pepper to taste

Line bottom of aluminum pie plate with aluminum foil, allowing extra to cover. Place fillets inside and top with butter/margarine, lemon juice and salt and pepper. Cover and place on grill. Cook for 8-10 minutes, or until fish is white and flaky.

Jay Ela
Franklin, Massachusetts

Banducci's Fish

Serves: 4
Prep Time: 45 minutes

fish fillets	**1 green bell pepper**
1 medium onion, diced	**salt and pepper to taste**
4 T. olive oil	**1 tsp. oregano**
5 garlic cloves, minced	**1 tsp. basil**
1 28-oz. can tomatoes	**1 tsp. rosemary, chopped**
1 red bell pepper	

Saute onion in olive oil. After 4 minutes, add garlic and cook for 2 more minutes. Add tomatoes with all other ingredients. Cook mixture for 20 minutes until all items blend together. Add fish fillets and completely cover them with sauce. (If you need a lot more sauce to cover, add either golden grain marinara sauce or tomato juice.) Cover skillet and cook for 20 minutes. Serve over rice.

William Banducci
Concord, California

Fish Bake

Serves: 3
Prep Time: 1 hour, 30 minutes

1 lb. frozen fish	**½ tsp. tarragon**
⅓ cup onion, chopped	**¼ tsp. thyme**
1 small garlic clove, chopped	**¼ tsp. salt**
	dash of pepper
2 tsp. butter	**¼ cup cornflake crumbs**

Place fillets in greased baking dish. Cook onion and garlic in butter. Stir in seasonings. Cook for 1 minute. Spread onion mixture over fish and top with crumbs. Bake at 500 degrees for 12 minutes.

Eric Shields
Fort Wayne, Indiana

Smoked Fish

Serves: 30
Prep Time: 11 hours

fish fillets	**½ lb. brown sugar**
garlic powder	**4 bay leaves, crushed**
6 qts. water	**3 lbs. kosher salt**
2 eggs	**vinegar**
½ pt. dark molasses	

Sprinkle garlic powder over top of water. Stir well. Add eggs (raw in shell), molasses, brown sugar and bay leaves. After all is mixed, put salt in a little at a time until eggs float. Make sure salt is dissolved every time. Soak fish in brine for 11 hours. Remove fish and smoke for 5-6 hours in medium-low wet wood. To can fish, remove skin and put in pint jars. Add 1 T. vinegar to each jar. Seal jars and pressure-cook for 90 minutes at 10-lbs. pressure.

Adelle Keech
Hale, Michigan

Tom's Fish Cakes

Serves: 5
Prep Time: 30 minutes

1 lb. fish fillets, boneless
5 large potatoes
cold water
2 T. onions, chopped
2 eggs
½ cup water
salt and pepper to taste

Peel and cut potatoes. Place potatoes in pot with fillets and cover with cold water. Boil until potatoes are done; drain. Mash fillets and potatoes together. Add onion, eggs and water. Mix and form into patties. Season with salt and pepper. Fry until golden brown.

Tom Boeckmann
Vinton, Iowa

Lemon Baked Fish

Serves: 6
Prep Time: 45 minutes

2 lbs. fish fillets	**1 T. dry mustard**
¼ tsp. paprika	**1 cup milk**
3 T. lemon juice	**½ cup bread crumbs**
salt and pepper to taste	**1 T. parsley, minced**
2 T. butter	
2 T. flour	

Cut fillets into serving-sized pieces and place in greased, baking dish. Sprinkle paprika, lemon juice and salt and pepper over fish. Combine butter, flour, dry mustard, salt and pepper and milk in saucepan. Cook until bubbly, then remove. Pour sauce over fillets. Sprinkle bread crumbs and parsley over fish. Bake at 350 degrees for 35 minutes.

Charles Stewart
Jeannette, Pennsylvania

Fish Casserole

Serves: 4-6
Prep Time: 45 minutes

2 cups fish chunks	**salt and pepper to taste**
1½ cups cracker crumbs	**½ cup melted butter**
1 cup celery, diced	**2 eggs, lightly beaten**
2 large onions, chopped	
½ cup parsley, chopped	
1 green pepper, seeded and chopped	

Combine fish, crumbs and vegetables. Add seasonings and mix with butter and eggs. Pour mixture into buttered casserole dish. Sprinkle bits of butter and extra crumbs over fish, if desired. Bake for 30 minutes at 375 degrees.

Robert Hill Jr.
Tullahoma, Tennessee

Beer-Battered Fish With Paprika

Serves: makes 1 cup batter
Prep Time: 8 minutes

> **fish fillets**
> 1 **cup flour**
> 1 **tsp. baking powder**
> 1 **tsp. salt**
> 1 **tsp. paprika**
> 1 **cup beer**
> 1 **egg**

Mix all dry ingredients, then add beer and egg. If batter is too thick, add more beer to desired thickness. Heat oil in electric fryer or deep skillet to about 375 degrees. Dip drip-dried fillets in batter and fry about 3-4 minutes (less for panfish fillets) or until flaky and crisp. (Don't overcook or you'll miss a lot of flavor.) If you have large or strong-flavored fillets, soak them in plain beer for 2-3 hours.

Randy Sautter
Crookston, Minnesota

Hickory And Cheese Fillets

Serves: 4 or more
Prep Time: 30 minutes

> **freshwater fish fillets**
> 1 **cup hickory or**
> **barbecue-hickory**
> **smoke sauce**
> 1 **onion, diced**
> 1-2 **cans cheddar cheese**
> **soup**

Layer fillets in 8x10-inch pan. Pour smoke sauce over fish fillets. Sprinkle onion over fish. Then pour cheddar cheese soup over everything. Cook in oven for about 20-30 minutes.

Ricky Kirk
Las Vegas, Nevada

Berry Hollow Fish Chowder

Serves: 6-8
Prep Time: 1 hour, 30 minutes

3½ cups fish, cubed
 4 bacon slices, chopped
 1 cup onion, chopped
 ¼ cup celery, chopped
 2 T. flour
 6 cups water

2 small turnips, peeled
   and chopped
2 medium potatoes, cubed
3 cups milk
   salt and pepper

Use large (preferably cast-iron) pot to fry bacon and render drippings. Add onions and celery. Saute until onions are clear. Stir in flour, but do not brown. Add water, turnips and potatoes. Cover and bring to a boil. Reduce heat to low and add milk and fish. Cover and cook for 1 hour, stirring occasionally. Add salt and pepper to taste.

Curtis Shuler
Eastover, South Carolina

Kentucky-Fried Fish

Serves: varies
Prep Time: 90 minutes

   fish fillets
 1 qt. buttermilk
   salt
   flour
   cornflakes, crushed

Cover fish fillets with buttermilk. Sprinkle 1 tsp. salt per pound of fish. Let stand for about 1 hour, then drain. Dip fillets in flour, then in crushed cornflakes. Fry in pan and serve with lemon or tartar sauce.

Ed Kowalski
Chicago, Illinois

Cajun Fish Sauce Picante

Serves: 8-10
Prep Time: 1 hour, 30 minutes

1 **lb. fish, diced**	1 **12-oz. can tomatoes**
¼ **cup olive oil**	1 **12-oz. can tomato sauce**
¼ **cup flour**	½ **cup green onions,**
½ **cup celery, chopped**	**chopped**
½ **cup bell peppers,**	**red pepper and salt to**
chopped	**taste**
4 **garlic cloves, chopped**	¼ **cup parsley**
1 **cup water**	

Heat oil. Add flour, stirring constantly until brown. Add celery, bell peppers and garlic. Saute until tender. Stir in water, tomatoes and tomato sauce. Bring to a boil. Add remaining ingredients and simmer for 1 hour. Serve over cooked rice with French bread.

Charles Cloudy
Orange, Texas

Oven-Baked Fish

Serves: 4
Prep Time: 15 minutes

1 **lb. fish fillets**
   freshly ground black
   pepper
⅓ **cup cornflake crumbs**
2 **T. oil**

Wash and dry fillets and cut into serving-sized pieces. Mix pepper with cornflake crumbs. Dip fish pieces in oil, then in cornflake crumbs. Arrange fillets in single layer in lightly oiled, shallow baking dish. Bake at 500 degrees for 10 minutes. Do not turn.

Nancy German
Pekin, Illinois

Dill And Lemon Baked Fish

Serves: 4
Prep Time: 30 minutes

- **4 fish fillets**
- **3 lemons**
- **1 stick butter**
- **1 dill sprig**
  salt and pepper to taste

Place each fillet in its own ovenproof dish. (Oval dishes with high sides works best.) Cut 2 lemons in half and squeeze the juice of half a lemon on each fillet. Melt butter and pour equal amounts in each dish. Now sprinkle dill over top of fillets and season with salt and pepper. Slice last lemon and lay a slice or two on top of each fillet. Bake at 350 degrees for 20 minutes.

Joe Gerencser Jr.
Milford, Indiana

Wahoo Steaks

Serves: 4
Prep Time: 40 minutes

- **2 large fish steaks,**
  (skinless)
  juice of ½ lemon
- **3 T. soy sauce**
- **3 T. water**
- **2 garlic cloves, pressed**
  olive oil
- **1 pkg. hollandaise sauce**

Cut steaks into medallions. Combine lemon juice, soy sauce, water and garlic cloves. Marinate fish in this mixture for at least 30 minutes, turning occasionally. Drain fish and pat dry. Dip fish in olive oil and broil for 3 minutes each side. Prepare hollandaise sauce and serve.

Gary Land
Clinton, Iowa

Fillets With Seasoned Brown Rice

Serves: 4
Prep Time: 20 minutes

1 **lb. fish fillets**	2 **T. lemon juice**
1½ **cups instant brown rice**	1¼ **cups water**
¼ **cup onion, chopped**	**butter**
1 **tsp. seasoning salt**	**dash of paprika**
1 **tsp. parsley, chopped**	
½ **tsp. ground thyme**	

Combine rice, onion, seasoning salt, parsley, thyme, lemon juice and water in 2-qt., glass casserole dish. Arrange fillets on top. Dot fillets with butter and sprinkle with paprika. Cover and microwave on high power for 10-12 minutes or until fish flakes easily. Let stand (covered) for 5 minutes.

Donald Kimberling
Omaha, Nebraska

Quick And Easy Camp Fish

Serves: 2
Prep Time: 15 minutes

1 **lb. fish fillets**
½ **stick butter**
¼ **tsp. garlic**
4 **carrots**
   salt and pepper

Melt butter in large skillet. Add garlic and bring to a boil. Add carrots, cooking until semi-tender. Cut fish into 3x3-inch chunks and add to carrots. Cook until fish flakes apart. Season with salt and pepper to taste.

Mark Zawodny
Hood River, Oregon

Fish And Cheese Soup

Serves: 4
Prep Time: 45 minutes

1 lb. fish fillets
¼ cup onions, finely chopped
¼ cup carrots, diced
¼ cup celery, diced
2 T. butter or margarine
¼ cup flour

¼ tsp. salt
dash of paprika
3 cups milk
1 14½-oz. can chicken broth
2 oz. processed American cheese, cubed

Cut fish into bite-sized pieces. Cook vegetables in butter until tender. Blend in flour, salt and paprika. Add milk and chicken broth. Cook and stir until thickened. Add fish and return to boiling. Reduce heat, cook and stir gently until fish flakes, about 5-8 minutes. Stir in cheese until melted. Serve.

Paul Trzeciak
Dayton, Ohio

Buttery Lemon Fish

Serves: 8
Prep Time: 20 minutes

8 fish, dressed
1 cup butter
⅓ cup lemon juice
¼ cup parsley, chopped
1 T. lemon peel, grated
1 T. salt
1 tsp. sugar
¼ tsp. pepper

Preheat broiler. On high heat, melt butter in 1-qt. saucepan. Stir in remaining ingredients. Place fish on rack in broiler pan and brush with butter mixture. Cook for about 5 minutes on each side, brushing often with butter mixture.

Edward Dunwiddie
Columbia, Montana

Fish Banquet

Serves: 3
Prep Time: 45 minutes

- **1 lb. fresh fish**
- **2 bacon slices**
- **2 potatoes, peeled and sliced**
- **1 onion, sliced**
- **salt and pepper**

Cut off a 12-inch square of aluminum foil. Lay 1 bacon slice on foil. Place fish on top of bacon and top with second bacon slice. Add potatoes and onion. Season with salt and pepper to taste. Wrap fish in foil, folding edges and ends over twice. Place upside down on another piece of foil, sealing again. Place packet in hot ashes or on top of grill away from direct flame. Cook for 15-20 minutes on each side after packet begins sizzling. Remove outer foil and serve.

Chad Bjorgaard
Viking, Minnesota

Ranch Fillets

Serves: 4
Prep Time: 15 minutes

- **8 fish fillets**
- **1¼ cups ranch-style dressing**
- **1 bag potato chips**
- **¾ cup cheese**

Pour dressing in 9x13-inch cake pan. Roll fillets in dressing, covering well. Pour shredded cheese over fillets. Crush potato chips and pour over top. Bake at 375 degrees for 20-25 minutes, or until fish is flaky. Then broil 2-3 minutes or until top is crunchy.

Ronald Goll
Brooklyn Park, Minnesota

Fish Camp Breakfast

Serves: 4-8
Prep Time: 30 minutes

- **2 lbs. fish fillets**
- **½ lb. bacon, diced**
- **1 medium onion, diced**
- **6-8 medium potatoes, diced**
- **½ tsp. garlic powder**
- **2 T. coarse lemon pepper**
- **Tabasco sauce to taste**
- **6-8 eggs**

In large skillet, cook bacon and onion until bacon is almost crisp. Add potatoes and cook until browned. Add garlic powder, lemon pepper, Tabasco sauce and fish fillets and cook for 2-5 minutes, stirring until evenly cooked. Finally, add eggs to above mixture, stirring constantly until eggs are cooked to desired consistency. Remove from fire and serve individual portions with lemon slices.

Steve Kennedy
Kansas City, Montana

Barbecue Fish

Serves: 4
Prep Time: 15 minutes

- **2 lbs. fish**
- **½ cup butter or margarine**
- **Worcestershire sauce**
- **¼ tsp. paprika**
- **1 T. lemon juice**
- **½ tsp. onion powder**
- **¼ tsp. garlic powder**
- **pepper to taste**

Combine all ingredients (except fish) for sauce. Brush sauce on both sides and inside of fish. Place fish into flat grill basket. Put basket on grill and cover. Cook for 12-15 minutes on medium heat, turning once. Serve with lemon wedges.

Chuck Pemberton
Phoenix, Arizona

Onion-Fish Scallop

Serves: 4
Prep Time: 30 minutes

2 lbs. fish fillets	¼ cup lemon juice
2 medium onions, thinly sliced	1 cup dry bread crumbs
¼ cup margarine	¼ tsp. paprika
salt and pepper to taste	2 T. margarine, melted
1 10½-oz. can cream of celery soup	

Saute onions in margarine until tender. Place half of onions in bottom of baking dish. Top with half of fish fillets. Lightly season with salt and pepper. Combine soup with lemon juice. Spread half of soup mixture over fish. Repeat with remaining ingredients. Combine bread crumbs with paprika and melted margarine and sprinkle over fish. Bake at 400 degrees for 20-30 minutes or until fish flakes easily.

Kenneth Schell
Mandan, North Dakota

Batter-Fried Fish

Serves: 2
Prep Time: 15 minutes

fresh fish fillets
1 egg
1 cup 7-Up
1 cup pancake mix
salt and pepper to taste

Heat deep-fat fryer. Beat egg and 7-Up together. Put pancake mix and salt and pepper in plastic bag. Dry fish and put in bag. Shake to coat fish. Then, dip coated fish in egg and 7-Up mixture. Place fish in hot grease. Fry only a few at a time.

Tom Boeckmann
Vinton, Iowa

Fish Fillets With Golden Mustard Sauce

Serves: varies
Prep Time: 1 hour, 15 minutes

fish fillets
2 **cups water**
1 **cup white wine**
1 **medium onion, thinly sliced**
1½ **tsp. parsley, minced**
1 **tsp. thyme**
½ **tsp. salt**
⅛ **tsp. pepper**
lemon juice
4 **T. butter**
3 **T. flour**
¾ **cup white wine**
3 **T. prepared mustard**
¼ **cup light cream**
salt and pepper to taste

Mix water, 1 cup wine, onion, parsley, thyme, salt and pepper in large pan. Allow sauce to simmer for 20-30 minutes. Rub fillets with salt and lemon juice. Simmer fillets in sauce over low heat for 10 minutes. Carefully watch so that fish doesn't break apart. For mustard sauce, make a roux of flour and butter. Stir over low heat until a light golden color. (Don't rush it or it will burn.) Slowly add 2 cups of poaching liquid ½ cup at a time. Season. Cook over low heat for 20 minutes until thickened. Add wine and simmer for 5 minutes. Remove from heat and add mustard and cream. Add more seasonings if needed. Place fish on serving plate. Garnish with parsley, lemon wedge and cherry tomatoes. Pass sauce in gravy boat. Serve with green beans and almonds.

Walter Squier
Portland, Connecticut

South-Of-The-Border Fish Casserole

Serves: 2-3
Prep Time: 45 minutes

12-16 oz. fish fillets, cooked
1 10¾-oz. can cream of
**   chicken soup**
**   water**
1 4-oz. can diced green
**   chilies**
½ tsp. instant minced
**   onion**

1 8-oz. pkg. corn chips
2 large tomatoes, thinly
**   sliced**
1 cup cheddar or Jack
**   cheese, shredded**

Preheat oven to 350 degrees. Grease 2-qt. baking dish.
Combine soup and ½ soup can water. Add chilies and minced
onions. Place half of corn chips in greased, casserole dish. Top
with half of fish. Add half of tomato slices, half of cheese and
half of soup mixture. Add remaining chips, then fish and
tomatoes. Add remaining soup mixture. Top with remaining
cheese. Bake for 35-40 minutes.

Walter Squier
Portland, Connecticut

Cornmeal Fillets

Serves: varies
Prep Time: 15-20 minutes

fish fillets
yellow cornmeal
pinch of salt
1 tsp. red pepper
grease

Mix yellow cornmeal, salt and red pepper. Roll fish in cornmeal
mixture. Heat 4-6 inches of grease. Using caution, test grease
by dropping a match in pan. If it ignites, it's ready. Fry fish until
it rises to surface. Flip and wait until golden brown.

Dennis Hughes
Deer Lodge, Montana

Stuffed Turban

Serves: 2
Prep Time: 15 minutes

2 4-oz. fillets, boned	**3 peppercorns**
water	**2 bay leaves**
clam juice	**8 asparagus spears**
white wine	**your choice of sauce**
salt	

Pour enough water, clam juice and wine into pan to cover turbans. Add pinch of salt, peppercorns and bay leaves. Heat to a simmer. Wrap each fillet around 2-3 asparagus spears, rolling with thin side toward thick side. Secure with toothpicks. Poach for 4-10 minutes or until done. Drain on napkin. Place on plate with your favorite sauce. Serve with wild rice.

Shawn Swenson
Torrance, California

Crispy Oven Fish

Serves: 4
Prep Time: 20-25 minutes

1 lb. fish fillets
2½ cups potato chips, finely crushed
½ cup Parmesan cheese, grated
½ cup mayonnaise or salad dressing
¼ cup lemon juice

Preheat oven to 375 degrees. Combine chips and cheese; set aside. In small bowl, combine mayonnaise and 2 T. lemon juice; set aside. Dip fish in remaining lemon juice, then mayonnaise mixture and chip mixture. Arrange in greased 13x9-inch baking dish. Bake 20 minutes or until fish flakes with fork.

Albert Kadet
Painesville, Ohio

Baked Stuffed Fish

Serves: 6
Prep Time: 1 hour, 30 minutes

1-4 lbs. fish
1 onion, chopped
1 T. parsley
2 T. butter
3 cups stale bread crumbs
1½ tsp. salt
⅛ tsp. pepper
2 eggs
½ cup boiling water

Brown onions and parsley in butter. Then, mix with crumbs, seasonings and eggs. Clean fish and season inside with salt and pepper. Using skewers, put stuffing in fish. Place fish on greased rack in broiler. Add boiling water and cover. (Leave valve on roaster open.) Bake at a temperature of 350 degrees for 1 hour, 15 minutes.

Donald Martin
North Port, Florida

Crispy Potato-Chip Fried Fish

Serves: 2-4
Prep Time: 30 minutes

1½ lbs. fish fillets, any kind
8-10 oz. rippled potato chips
2 eggs
¼ cup cooking oil

Crush potato chips in sealable plastic bag with rolling pin. Beat eggs in small bowl. Dip one fillet at a time in egg and drop in bag of potato chips. Shake until fillet is covered with chips. Place in hot oil and cook until both sides are golden brown. Drain on paper towels.

Jay Ela
Franklin, Massachusetts

Black Bean Fish

Serves: 4
Prep Time: 45-60 minutes

1 **3-lb. fish fillet, firm white meat**	**canola oil**
4 **T. black bean, crushed**	**green onion, chopped**
2 **garlic cloves, mashed**	**dash of MSG**
½ **tsp. salt**	6 **T. water**
½ **tsp. sugar**	1 **T. soy sauce**
	1 **T. cornstarch**

Combine black bean, garlic, salt and sugar. Fry fish in canola oil, then add black bean mixture and turn fish until done. Remove fish from pan. Add green onion, MSG, water and soy sauce. Thicken sauce with cornstarch. Pour sauce over fish.

Chris Seung
Mukilteo, Washington

Fun Fish Chowder

Serves: 4
Prep Time: 30 minutes

1 **lb. fish fillets, diced**
5 **bacon slices, diced**
1 **small onion, diced**
2 **cups water**
2 **medium potatoes, diced**
  salt and pepper
2 **cups milk**
½ **cup carrots, cooked**

In frying pan, brown bacon. Add onion and cook until tender. Add water, potatoes and fish. Season with salt and pepper to taste. Cook over low heat until potatoes are tender (approximately 15-30 minutes). Add milk and carrots, heating thoroughly. For a thicker chowder, add a light roux.

Leslie Gaines
Mount Vernon, Texas

Broiled Fillets

Serves: 4
Prep Time: 30 minutes

1½ lbs. fish fillets	lemon pepper
1 stick butter	seasoned salt
½ tsp. lemon juice	paprika
seasoned black pepper	parsley flakes

Place fillets on aluminum foil. Broil until almost done. Combine butter and lemon juice and heat until butter melts. Remove fillets from broiler and baste with melted butter mixture. Shake seasoned black pepper, lemon pepper, seasoned salt and paprika over fish. Return fillets to broiler and lightly brown. (Do not overcook.) Garnish with parsley flakes and serve.

John Stark
Eldon, Missouri

Fish In Beer Batter

Serves: 4-6
Prep Time: 15 minutes

  fish fillets
1 cup flour
⅛ tsp. salt
1 egg
1 T. vegetable oil
⅜ cup milk
¼ cup beer

Sift flour and salt in medium bowl. Combine egg and oil in separate dish. Make a "well" in center of dry mixture and pour in egg mixture; then slowly fold in flour. Gradually add milk and beer. Mix until smooth batter forms. Cover bowl and set aside in cool place for 30 minutes. Coat fish and fry in oil for 4-5 minutes, or until crisp and brown.

Michael Bailey
Nineveh, Indiana

Microwaved Fish Fiesta

Serves 5-6
Prep Time: 4-5 minutes

1 lb. fish fillets	**1 tomato, chopped**
1 tsp. salt	**1 T. lime juice**
¼ tsp. pepper	**1 T. vegetable oil**
1 small onion, sliced	**1 T. parsley, snipped**

If fish fillets are large, cut into 5-6 serving-sized pieces. Place fish in ungreased, square, glass baking dish. Season with salt and pepper. Cover and microwave until fish is almost done, about 4 minutes. Top with onion and tomato and drizzle with lime juice and oil. Sprinkle parsley over top and cover. Microwave until vegetables are crisp-tender.

Sam Tackett
Duff, Tennessee

Fish In Foil

Serves: 4
Prep Time: 10 minutes

4 fish fillets or steaks
4 T. butter
4 Swiss cheese slices
1 onion, sliced
2 carrots, sliced
  dill to taste
  salt and pepper to taste

Tear 4 strips of aluminum foil, place 1 T. butter in middle of each strip, then place fillets on butter. Put cheese slice on top of fish, then ¼ of onion and ¼ of carrots. Sprinkle dried dill and salt and pepper over fillets. Seal foil over fish and cook for 15-20 minutes at 400 degrees.

Charles Everts
Ogden, Utah

Grilled Fish Fillets

Serves: 6
Prep Time: 1 hour, 20 minutes

6 fish fillets, ¾ inch thick
½ cup butter or margarine
¼ cup lemon juice
1 T. Worcestershire sauce
½ tsp. seasoned salt
½ tsp. paprika
¼ tsp. red pepper

Place fillets in large, shallow dish. Combine remaining ingredients in saucepan and cook, stirring constantly until butter melts. Pour marinade over fish. Cover and marinate for 1 hour in refrigerator, turning once. Drain fillets, reserving marinade. Place fillets in fish basket. Grill over hot coals for 5 minutes on each side or until fish flakes easily when tested with fork. Baste often with marinade.

Charles Fish
Smithville, Tennessee

Flaked-Fish Hash And Tomato Soup

Serves: 2
Prep Time: 30 minutes

2 cups fish, flaked
several bacon strips, diced
2 cups potatoes, boiled, chopped and cold
1 T. onion and chives, minced
salt and pepper to taste
1 can tomato soup

Panfry bacon until crisp. Mix potatoes, onion and chives and salt and pepper. Add fried bacon bits to potato mixture along with fish, stirring to blend. Place mixture in hot bacon drippings and fry until brown. (Do not stir.) Fold over and serve like an omelet. Pour hot tomato soup over top.

John Linstman
Fulton, Indiana

Tomato And Fish

Serves: 5
Prep Time: 20 minutes

1⅞ **lbs. fish fillets**	**salt and pepper to taste**
1¼ **lbs. tomatoes, chopped**	1¼ **T. butter**
1¼ **T. onion, minced**	1¼ **T. lemon juice**
¼ **tsp. basil**	⅓ **cup water**
⅓ **tsp. dill weed**	
cooking oil	

Combine tomatoes, onion, basil and dill weed; set aside. Brush fillets with oil and season with salt and pepper. Place tomato mixture in center of each fillet. Melt butter in skillet. Cook and stir onion until tender. Place fish in skillet. Add lemon juice and water. Simmer until tender (about 10 minutes).

Joseph Trojanowski
Fort Worth, Texas

Sweet-Tart Dill Glaze

Serves: several
Prep Time: 20 minutes

fish fillets	4 **oz. favorite prepared**
½ **cup dry white wine**	**mustard**
8 **oz. lemon juice**	2 **oz. pure honey**
2 **T. dill weed**	

In saucepan over low heat, pour wine, lemon juice and dill weed, stirring constantly. Add mustard and honey. Mix thoroughly until bubbling. Remove from heat and let cool. Prepare your favorite fish by baking. Approximately 5 minutes before serving, apply glaze to each piece of fish and continue baking for 5 minutes. Serve individual portions, garnished with pineapple or orange slices.

Steve Kennedy
Kansas City, Montana

Fish Chowder

Serves: 4
Prep Time: 45 minutes

½ **cup fish, diced**
5-6 **large potatoes, diced**
1 **large onion, diced**
1 **celery stalk, diced**
8 **cups milk**
¼ **cup margarine or butter**
salt and pepper
instant mashed potatoes

Boil potatoes until soft, then drain. Saute onion and celery while potatoes are cooking. Combine fish, potatoes, celery, onion, milk and margarine. Add salt and pepper to taste. Cook over medium-low heat, stirring frequently. (Be careful not to burn.) Minutes before serving, add instant potatoes to create desired thickness.

Doc Smyk
Jacksonville, Florida

Sauteed Fish

Serves: 4
Prep Time: 20 minutes

1 **lb. fish**
1 **cup milk**
1 **egg**
½ **tsp. salt**
½ **tsp. pepper**

pinch of garlic
2 **cups flour**
1 **cup oil**
1 **cup wine**
1 **tsp. lemon juice**

Mix milk, egg, salt, pepper and garlic together. Dip fish in this mixture, then coat with flour. Heat oil until hot. Put fish in hot oil for 2 minutes, making sure to turn while frying. Fry until golden brown. Drain oil from fish. Add wine and lemon juice to fish.

Eric Eckenrode
Dover, Pennsylvania

Buttered Microwave Fish Fillets

Serves: 4
Prep Time: 12 minutes

1 lb. fish fillets	**2 T. cornstarch**
3 T. butter	**¼ cup slivered almonds**
2 T. lemon juice	

In glass dish, melt butter. Add lemon juice, cornstarch and almonds and stir. Add fish and coat well with butter mixture. Cover with plastic wrap and microwave on high for 4 minutes or until fish flakes easily. Let stand for 2-3 minutes (covered) before serving.

Dale Meyer
Kensett, Iowa

Vegetable-Baked Fish

Serves: 2
Prep Time: 30 minutes

1 lb. fish fillets
½ cup zucchini, sliced
1 green pepper, sliced
1 tomato, sliced
1 onion, sliced
¼ tsp. salt
⅛ tsp. pepper
¼ cup water
1 T. butter
⅛ tsp. paprika

Place half of vegetables in baking dish. Season fish with salt and pepper. Place fish on top of vegetables. Cover fish with remaining vegetables. Add water, then dot with butter and sprinkle with paprika. Bake at 350 degrees for 20-25 minutes.

Joseph Trojanowski
Fort Worth, Texas

INDEX

BAKED FISH
baked bass, 45
baked bluegills, 60
baked fillet of walleye, 144
baked fillets, 153
baked fish, 154
baked fish fillets, 155
baked fish in cheese sauce, 97
baked fish steaks, 164
baked lake michigan trout, 134
baked perch, 92
baked pike fillets, 87
baked salmon, 100
baked salmon dijon, 103
baked salmon hash, 103
baked salmon steaks, 113
baked sole with broccoli, 118
baked striped bass with clams, 119
baked stuffed fish, 183
baked stuffed trout, 123
baked trout with cheese, 124
breakfast baked snook, 117
cheese fish bake, 156
crispy oven fish, 182
crunchy oven-fried crappie, 74
dan's baked fish fillets, 156
dill and lemon baked fish, 174
fish and vegetable bake, 151
fish bake, 168
fish casserole, 170
fish in foil, 186
fish roll-ups, 157

foil-baked fish, 79
fresh catch parmesan, 158
gourmet trout bake, 135
hickory and cheese fillets, 171
larry's bluefish bake, 57
lemon baked fish, 170
onion-fish scallop, 179
oven-baked fish, 173
quick baked walleye fillets, 141
red snapper baked with oranges and pineapple, 96
red wine fish, 153
red-headed spicy crappie grill bake, 72
savory outdoor baked fish, 166
seafarer's dinner, 167
south-of-the-border fish casserole, 181
vegetable-baked fish, 190

BASS
7-up bass, 46
baked bass, 45
bass fillets with mornay sauce, 43
bass italiano, 47
bass 'n' peppers, 53
bass with dijon & peppercorn sauce, 54
broiled bass, 43
broiled bass amandine, 49
cajun bass, 52
cajun bass and rice, 50
cajun bass fillets, 51
fried bass fingers, 52

largemouth delight, 48
lemon pepper bass, 44
mexican bass fillets, 44
pimiento glazed bass, 55
sea bass amandine, 51
smoked bass fillet, 55
southern-fried bass, 49
southern-grilled bass, 56
steamed bass, 54
stuffed bass, 47
tart & tangy bass, 53
terry's bass courtbouillon, 46
tj's blackened bass, 56
walnut fried bass, 45
white bass vegetable stir-fry, 48

BLUEFISH
broiled bay bluefish, 57
larry's bluefish bake, 57

BLUEGILL
baked bluegills, 60
bluegill salad, 59
bluegill with zucchini, 58
fried bluegills, 59
panfish marinade, 58
quick and easy beer battered
  bluegills, 60

BOILED FISH
boiled fish, 165
boiled perch fillets, 91

BROILED FISH
broiled bass, 43
broiled bass amandine, 49
broiled bay bluefish, 57
broiled brown trout, 127
broiled fillets, 185
broiled fish dijon, 166
broiled fish fillets, 155
broiled mexican catfish fillets,
  66
broiled salmon steaks, 102
broiled walleye, 143

buttery lemon fish, 176
char-broiled salmon steaks, 98
meal-in-one seafood platter, 159
ranch fillets, 177
wahoo steaks, 174

CAJUN
cajun bass, 52
cajun bass and rice, 50
cajun bass fillets, 51
cajun catfish, 63
cajun fish sauce picante, 173
cajun-style crappies, 71
fish creole, 145

CATFISH
broiled mexican catfish fillets, 66
cajun catfish, 63
catfish stew, 62
catfish veracruz, 64
crispy catfish, 66
crispy fried catfish, 61
fried catfish, 65
lasoy catfish, 67
marinated catfish, 61
sesame parmesan catfish, 62
southern catfish stew, 63
spicy catfish, 67
spicy hot catfish (grilled), 65

CHOWDER
berry hollow fish chowder, 172
connecticut chowder, 148
fish chowder, 157, 189
fun fish chowder, 184
pam's head chowder, 69
salmon chowder, 108

COD
bailey's fish and chips, 70
pam's head chowder, 69
parmesan baked cod, 70
poached cod, 68
poached lemon fish, 69
salt cod and peanut stew, 68

Index

CRAPPIE
buttermilk crappies, 73
cajun-style crappies, 71
crappie delight, 71
crunchy oven-fried crappie, 74
cucumber crappies, 75
healthy and quick crappies, 72
italian fried fish, 75
lawrey's-adkins' crappie, 74
red-headed spicy crappie grill
  bake, 72

FISH CAKES
fish cakes, 150
tom's fish cakes, 169

FLOUNDER
bar-b-qued door mat, 76
flounder provencale, 77
prawn rolled flounder, 76

FRIED FISH
banducci's fish, 168
batter-dipped perch, 92
batter-fried fish, 179
beer batter fillets, 144
beer batter fish, 149
beer batter sturgeon, 121
beer-battered fish with paprika,
  171
black bean fish, 184
cornmeal fillets, 181
crispy catfish, 66
crispy fried catfish, 61
crispy potato-chip fried fish, 183
deep-fried perch fillets, 93
deep-fried sea trout, 124
delicious fish patties, 158
fillets pan-fried, 163
fish and asparagus bundles, 154
fish cakes, 150
fish camp breakfast, 178
fish in beer batter, 185
fried bass fingers, 52
fried bluegills, 59
fried catfish, 65

italian fried fish, 75
kentucky-fried fish, 172
pan-fried brook trout, 130
pan-fried trout, 123
pancake-battered fish, 161
quick and easy beer battered
  bluegills, 60
quick and easy camp fish, 175
sauteed fish, 189
southern-fried bass, 49
southern-fried trout, 129
striper deep-fry, 120
stu beer-batter perch, 93
sweet-tart dill glaze, 188
tom's fish cakes, 169
walnut fried bass, 45

GAR
gar balls, 78
garfish balls, 78

GRILLED FISH
bar-b-qued door mat, 76
barbecue fish, 178
barbecued fish fillets, 148
barbecued salmon, 99, 109
barbecued walleye fillets, 142
easy barbecue fish, 167
fish banquet, 177
fish in foil over fire, 151
grilled fennel-stuffed salmon, 108
grilled fillets, 152
grilled fish, 159
grilled fish fillets, 187
grilled fish in foil, 163
grilled hawaiian fish, 83
grilled pike, 85
grilled poached walleye, 145
grilled red snapper, 96
grilled salmon, 105
grilled trout with crab stuffing, 136
grilled weakfish with
  vegetables, 146
grilled yellowtail, 147
jeff's barbecued trout, 129
john's grilled salmon, 110

Index

marinated grilled striper, 119
pepper grilled salmon, 110
salmon on the grill, 114
savory grilled salmon, 104
southern-grilled bass, 56
spicy hot catfish (grilled), 65
zesty grilled trout, 132

HALIBUT
a parcel for the halibut, 80
fish kabobs, 81
foil-baked fish, 79
halibut kabobs, 81
rosemary's halibut, 79

ITALIAN
bass italiano, 47
italian fried fish, 75
walleye italiano, 142

MACKEREL
steamed mackerel with meat, 82
sweet and sour chinese fish, 82

MAHI MAHI
grilled hawaiian fish, 83
"kipper's" fish, 84
mahi mahi magic, 83

MICROWAVED FISH
buttered microwave fish fillets, 190
fillets with seasoned brown rice, 175
microwaved fish fiesta, 186
microwaved trout and mushrooms, 133
steamed walleye in microwave, 143

MISCELLANEOUS
cajun fish sauce picante, 173
courtbouillon, 150
fish and cheese soup, 176

flaked-fish hash and tomato soup, 187
ma's pickled fish, 160
panfish marinade, 58
pickled fish, 161
quick swiss fish rolls, 152
smoked fillets, 164
smoked fish, 169
tomato and fish, 188
warm fish salad with blue cheese, 149

NORTHERN
baked pike fillets, 87
fish and chips, 88
grilled pike, 85
northern pike croquet, 88
pike ala-mert, 86
pike nuggets, 85
poor man's lobster my way, 87

ORANGE ROUGHY
henry's spicy roughy, 89
orange roughy rollups, 89

ORIENTAL
sweet and sour chinese fish, 82
white bass vegetable stir-fry, 48

PERCH
baked perch, 92
batter-dipped perch, 92
boiled perch fillets, 91
crispy perch, 90
deep-fried perch fillets, 93
ginger ale perch, 90
perch scampi, 91
stu beer-batter perch, 93

POACHED FISH
fish fillets with golden mustard sauce, 180
grilled poached walleye, 145
poached cod, 68

poached fillets in cheese sauce, 160
poached fish, 162
poached lemon fish, 69
stuffed turbans, 182

REDFISH
redfish in orange, 94

RED MULLET
red mullet with cognac, 95

RED SNAPPER
baked fish in cheese sauce, 97
grilled red snapper, 96
red snapper baked with oranges and pineapple, 96

SALMON
baked salmon, 100
baked salmon dijon, 103
baked salmon hash, 103
baked salmon steaks, 113
barbecued salmon, 99, 109
basic canned fish, 101
broiled salmon steaks, 102
canned smoked salmon, 115
char-broiled salmon steaks, 98
crispy salmon steaks, 101
dry mix for smoked salmon, 112
great lakes canned salmon, 102
grilled fennel-stuffed salmon, 108
grilled salmon, 105
jerked salmon, 111
john's grilled salmon, 110
kipper morning, 113
oven-steamed salmon, 98
pepper grilled salmon, 110
salmon ala foil, 99
salmon balls in mushroom sauce, 109
salmon chowder, 108
salmon continental, 105
salmon dip, 115
salmon gourmet, 107

salmon on the grill, 114
salmon patties, 104
salmon soup, 111
salmon stuffing, 100
savory grilled salmon, 104
seafood omelet, 114
smoked fish dutches, 106
smoked salmon, 112
smoked salmon spread, 107

SHARK
shark brochettes, 116
shark fillets, 116

SNOOK
breakfast baked snook, 117

SOLE
baked sole with broccoli, 118
nordick stuffed fillet ala lisa, 118

STEAMED FISH
beer steamed lake trout, 134
oven-steamed salmon, 98
steamed bass, 54
steamed mackerel with meat, 82
steamed walleye in microwave, 143

STEW
catfish stew, 62
salt cod and peanut stew, 68
southern catfish stew, 63

STRIPER
baked striped bass with clams, 119
marinated grilled striper, 119
striped fish supreme, 120
striper deep-fry, 120

STUFFED FISH
baked stuffed fish, 183
baked stuffed trout, 123
eddy's stuffed trout, 133

grilled fennel-stuffed salmon, 108

grilled trout with crab stuffing, 136

nordick stuffed fillet ala lisa, 118

stuffed bass, 47

stuffed turbans, 182

STURGEON

beer batter sturgeon, 121

SWORDFISH

orange and basil marinated swordfish, 122

zesty tomato fillets, 122

TROUT

all there is, trout, 125

bacon lakers, 126

baked lake michigan trout, 134

baked rainbow trout, 126

baked stuffed trout, 123

baked trout with cheese, 124

barbecued trout, 127

beer steamed lake trout, 134

broiled brown trout, 127

campfire lake trout, 131

deep-fried sea trout, 124

eddy's stuffed trout, 133

gourmet trout bake, 135

grilled trout, 128

grilled trout with crab stuffing, 136

jeff's barbecued trout, 129

jim's baked trout, 137

lake trout ala lemon-beer, 128

lakeside trout, 125

microwaved trout and mushrooms, 133

pan-fried brook trout, 130

pan-fried trout, 123

pepper trout, 131

ron's trout amandine, 137

smoked trout, 130

southern-fried trout, 129

steelhead supreme, 132

trout amandine, 136

trout in foil, 135

zesty grilled trout, 132

TUNA

carl's supreme tuna surprise, 139

tuna surprise, 138

tuna swiss pie, 138

WALLEYE

baked fillet of walleye, 144

barbecued walleye fillets, 142

beer batter fillets, 144

broiled walleye, 143

broiled walleye fillets, 140

fish creole, 145

grilled poached walleye, 145

quick baked walleye fillets, 141

steamed walleye in microwave, 143

walleye fish sticks, 140

walleye italiano, 142

walleye with almonds, 141

WEAKFISH

grilled weakfish with vegetables, 146

WHITEFISH

freshwater whitefish, 165

whitefish soup, 162

YELLOWTAIL

grilled yellowtail, 147

Contributing Members

Abreo, Terry
Lutcher, LA, 46, 56
Akira, A.W.
Knoxville, TN, 49
Allphin, Buddy
New Richmond, OH, 54
Arrant, Kevin
Sarasota, FL, 52, 94
Bailey, Michael
Nineveh, IN, 70, 142, 162, 185
Baker, Harold
Colorado Springs, CO, 152
Banducci, William
Concord, CA, 76, 168
Belshe, Gary
Lakeside, OR, 112, 115
Berge, Michael
North Bend, OR, 55, 103
Bigall, Mike
Redding, CA, 54
Bjorgaard, Chad
Viking, MN, 166, 177
Boeckmann, Tom
Vinton, IA, 169, 179
Boehmke, Douglas
Sheridan, IL, 87
Brant, T.J.
Olympia, WA, 111
Breiner, Dennis
Wichita, KS, 149, 158
Brown, Teresa
Evansville, WY, 135, 141
Buckles, Joe
Michigan Center, MI, 103
Bumpus, Steve
Mason, MI, 85
Cepress, James
Roseville, MN, 107, 108
Chapman, Foster William III
Minnetonka, MN, 141, 163
Chastain, Scott
Haines City, FL, 77, 101
Chmiel, Jeffrey
Buffalo, NY, 88, 149

Cloudy, Charles
Orange, TX, 173
Conley, Barb
Louisville, NE, 153, 155
Cook, Susan
Holcomb, NY, 62, 63, 124, 127, 129, 165
Craig, John
Shelocta, PA, 142, 157
Crowley, Don, Sr.
Milford, MA, 163, 164
Daniel, Bill
Marshall, AR, 66, 67
Dodson, Mark
Corrales, NM, 128
Dominquez, Jeff
Vacaville, CA, 121, 129
Douglas, S.
Roslindale, MA, 125
Downs, Gene
Ozark, AL, 49, 56
Dunn, Leo
Park Forest, IL, 116, 124
Dunwiddie, Edward
Columbia, MT, 176
Eastridge, James
North East, MD, 48, 120
Eck, Conrad
Ellenville, NY, 75, 91
Eckenrode, Eric
Dover, PA, 68, 189
Eisenhauer, T.
Rockaway, NY, 51
Ela, Jay
Franklin, MA, 167, 183
Everts, Charles
Ogden, UT, 123, 186
Fee, James
St. Paul, MN, 43
Filsinger, Jeannine and Richard
Honolulu, HI, 83
Filsinger, Richard
Honolulu, HI, 79
Fish, Charles
Smithville, TN, 61, 187

Gadzik, Nate
  Mesa, AZ, 65, 114
Gaines, Leslie
  Mount Vernon, TX, 159, 184
Gardner, Lee
  Corvallis, OR, 80, 81
Gerencser, Joe, Jr.
  Milford, IN, 114, 174
German, Nancy
  Pekin, IL, 43, 173
Glover, Mike
  Dallas, TX, 74
Goll, Ronald
  Brooklyn Park, MN, 137, 177
Gray, Jerry
  Jackson, WY, 127, 131
Grimes, Paul
  Rio Rancho, NM, 68, 109
Guertner, Bill
  Eatonville, WA, 98
Harris, Art
  Jupiter, FL, 78, 117
Headley, Joanna
  Miami, FL, 82
Henley, Bill, Jr.
  Hopewell, VA, 66, 119
Henry, Sam
  Ogden, VT, 89
Hill, Robert, Jr.
  Tullahoma, TN, 155, 170
Hixson, Linda
  Barling, AR, 61, 62
Hodgdon, James
  Kansas City, MO, 55, 110
Hoffman, Charles
  Albany, NY, 139
Hughes, Dennis
  Deer Lodge, MT, 161, 181
Hummel, Danny
  Essex, IA, 156
Irish, Larry
  Niantic, CT, 57, 69
Jackson, Mildred
  Williston, SC, 120
Jensen, Elmer
  Eagle River, WI, 90, 151

Jensen, Virgil
  Battle Lake, MN, 156
Jones, Patricia
  South Daytona, FL, 152
Kadet, Albert
  Painesville, OH, 48, 182
Keech, Adelle
  Hale, MI, 169
Kekic, Kevin
  Tucson, AZ, 71
Kennedy, Steve
  Kansas City, MT, 178, 188
Kimberling, Donald
  Omaha, NE, 122, 175
Kirk, Ricky
  Las Vegas, NV 111, 171
Knight, David
  Waxahachie, TX, 46
Knittle, Edward
  Lakewood, CO, 84
Kowalski, Ed
  Chicago, IL, 109, 172
Krise, Gordon
  Harpursville, NY, 92, 133
Kurth, Brook
  Indianapolis, IN, 87
Ladd, Charlie
  Bowling Green, OH, 85, 157
Land, Gary
  Clinton, IA, 174
Largent, Thomas
  Beaverton, MI, 131, 135
Larimore, Stephen
  Louisville, KY, 51
Leachman, Sean
  North Highlands, CA, 44, 45
Lepak, Walt
  Meriden, CT, 125
Linstman, John
  Fulton, IN, 59, 187
Loberg, Edwin
  Annandale, VA, 130
Lozak, Michael
  Parlin, NJ, 67, 136
Malinowski, J.
  Royal Oak, MI, 69

Marino, Christopher
  Staten Island, NY, 102
Martin, Chad
  Redwood Falls, MN, 105
Martin, Donald
  North Port, FL, 183
McKinney, Patricia
  Carthage, MO, 126
Medley, Eugene
  Noble, LA, 45
Meyer, Dale
  Kensett, IA, 167, 190
Miller, Warren
  Princeton, MN, 154
Mills, Barbara
  Clinton, WA, 106, 112
Moline, Mario, Jr.
  Brownsville, TX, 76
Monten, Gordon, Jr.
  Belfair, WA, 99
Moore, Gary
  Eltopia, WA, 104
Musgrave, Ronald
  Darby, MT, 53, 132
Nagy, Tracy
  Cuyahoga Falls, OH, 107, 154
Nieman, Mark
  Hawarden, IA, 145
Olexa, Matthew
  Bloomsburg, PA, 158
Paleck, Steve
  Rapid City, SD, 140
Pasch, Ron
  Freeport, IL, 92, 143
Pelliching, David
  Hammond, LA, 58
Pemberton, Chuck
  Phoenix, AZ, 64, 178
Phillips, Edward
  Troy, NY, 133, 136
Pontiff, Paul
  Baldwin, LA, 78
Posseneau, Kenneth
  Wisconsin Rapids, WI, 115
Ratliff, Darren
  Tauares, FL, 52

Roe, William, Jr.
  Newark, DE, 88
Rooney, Richard
  Laramie, WY, 126
Rose, David
  Traverse City, MN, 128
Rottler, William
  Fountain, MI, 101, 134
Ruhl, Tom
  Princeton, WI, 113, 144
Sautter, Randy
  Crookston, MN, 145, 171
Saver, James, Jr.
  Larsen, WI, 140
Schaffer, Milbert
  Pierre, SD, 100
Schell, Kenneth
  Mandan, ND, 60, 179
Schmaltz, Mark
  Niles, MI, 108
Schneiderman, Robert
  Flushing, NY, 113
Schrauth, Scott
  Ridgewood, NY, 57, 96
Scott, Richard
  Conneaut, OH, 59, 143
Seung, Chris
  Mukilteo, WA, 105, 184
Seymour, Richard
  Julian, CA, 79, 89
Shaver, Jeffery
  Wayland, NY, 58
Sheppard, Mike
  Escatawapa, MS, 53, 96
Shields, Eric
  Fort Wayne, IN, 138, 168
Shuler, Curtis
  Eastover, SC, 172
Sinclair, Lisa
  Salem, NJ, 118, 146
Slack, Mark
  Eureka, CA, 104
Smyk, Doc
  Jacksonville, FL, 165, 189
Sontag, James
  Pocatello, ID, 100, 144

Squier, Walter
  Portland, CT, 148, 160, 180, 181
Stark, John
  Eldon, MO, 73, 185
Stewart, Charles
  Jeannette, PA, 151, 170
Stewart, James
  Inkster, MI, 90, 93
Stover, Mike
  Dallas, TX, 75
Strayer, Glenn
  Algona, IA, 72, 86
Streit, Todd
  Pasadena, CA, 70, 116
Strunk, James
  Philadelphia, PA, 50, 97, 118,
  166
Sumter, Gynita
  Elgin, SC, 63
Swartz, Steven
  Clearbrook, VA, 138, 150
Swenson, Shawn
  Torrance, CA, 153, 182
Tackett, Sam
  Duff, TN, 186
Tapanes, Oswaldo
  Miami, FL, 83, 147
Terrano, Joe
  Port Republic, VA, 47
Thompson, Delbert
  Woodland, WA, 99
Timmerman, Gerald
  Bishop, CA, 148
Tolen, Joe
  Philadelphia, PA, 95
Trnka, Bob
  Waseca, MN, 102, 160

Trojanowski, Joseph
  Fort Worth, TX, 162, 188, 190
Trout, William
  Des Moines, IA, 161
Trzeciak, Paul
  Dayton, OH, 176
Uncapher, James
  Johnstown, PA, 137
Volk, Stan
  Crestline, OH, 159
Wertman, Nelson
  Romulus, NY, 98, 134
West, Cory
  Yuba City, CA, 132
West, Jim
  Coldwater, MS, 44
Wicke, John William
  Frankfort, MI, 110
Wilburn, Shirley
  San Antonio, TX, 72
Wilson, Al
  Port Neches, TX, 150, 164
Wilson, LeeRoy
  Omaha, NE, 74
Wirth, John
  Plainview, NY, 119, 122
Wiskirski, Leo
  Summit Hill, PA, 60, 123
Wood, Daniel
  Pringle, SD, 71, 130
Woods, Roy
  Big Rapids, MI, 65
Zajkowski, Robert, Sr.
  Hartford, MI, 91, 93
Zawodny, Mark
  Hood River, OR, 175

SEND US YOUR FISH RECIPE

Title:_____

Serves:_____

Prep Time:_____

Ingredients:

_____
_____
_____
_____
_____
_____
_____
_____
_____

Directions:

fold here

_____
_____
_____
_____
_____
_____
_____
_____
_____
_____
_____
_____
_____
_____
_____
_____
_____
_____

Your NAFC Member #_____

Your Name_____

Address_____

City/State/Zip_____

North American Fishing Club
12301 Whitewater Drive
P.O. Box 3403
Minnetonka, MN 55343

(tape or staple here)

SEND US YOUR FISH RECIPE

Title: _____

Serves: _____

Prep Time: _____

Ingredients:

_____

_____

_____

_____

_____

_____

_____

_____

_____

Directions:

_____ fold here

_____

_____

_____

_____

_____

_____

_____

_____

_____

_____

_____

_____

_____

_____

_____

_____

_____

Your NAFC Member # _____

Your Name _____

Address _____

City/State/Zip _____

- -

North American Fishing Club
12301 Whitewater Drive
P.O. Box 3403
Minnetonka, MN 55343

A Great Gift Idea...

The NAFC Members' Cookbook!

Order extra copies of the 1993 NAFC Members' Cookbook
for your friends and family. They make great gifts
– fun to read and practical as well!

You'll also like to have a second copy to keep
at the cabin or in with your camping gear.

Send your order in now and get yours at the
special Member's price of only $9.95 each.
(Non-members pay $14.95)

Send me _____ copies of the 1993 NAFC Members' Cookbook.
I'm enclosing $9.95 each (non-members pay $14.95).
Include $1.50 per order for Postage and Handling.

If paying by Check or Money Order, send this form in
an envelope with your payment to: NAFC Members' Cookbook,
P.O. Box 3408, Minnetonka, MN 55343.
Charge customers may cut out this page, fold and mail.
(Don't forget to put on a stamp)

Payment Method:
__ Check or M.O.
__ MasterCard
__ Visa
__ Discover Card

Card # _____

Exp. Date _____

Signature _____

Name _____ Member # _____

Address _____

City/State/Zip _____

CB93

North American Fishing Club
12301 Whitewater Drive
P.O. Box 3408
Minnetonka, MN 55343

Fishermen belong in the NAFC...
and it's so *simple* to join!
Cut out, fold and mail the card below.

‑ ➤

- *North American Fisherman* magazine
- *Fishing Club Journal* newsletter
- Trade-A-Trips with fellow members
- Fishing Reports on guides/outfitters
- Approved Guides, Camps & Charter Services booklet
- Free Fishing Trips & Gear
- New Product & Field Test Reports
- Products & Service Discounts
- Your picture in Member Photos
- Meeting Place, Bits & Pieces and much, much more!

fold her

ENROLLMENT FORM

Count me in . . .

I want to increase my fishing skill and enjoyment.

Here are my $18 annual dues for charter membership in the North American Fishing Club. I understand my membership will start immediately upon receipt of this application and continue for 12 months.

Name‑‑‑‑‑‑‑‑‑‑‑‑‑‑‑‑‑‑‑‑‑‑‑‑‑‑‑‑‑
PLEASE PRINT

Address‑‑‑‑‑‑‑‑‑‑‑‑‑‑‑‑‑‑‑‑‑‑‑‑‑

City‑‑‑‑‑‑‑‑‑‑‑‑‑ State‑‑‑‑‑ Zip‑‑‑‑‑

Check One:

☐ Check for $18 enclosed
☐ Bill my MasterCard/VISA

Credit Card No. ‑‑‑‑‑‑‑‑‑‑‑‑‑‑ Exp. Date‑‑‑‑

Signature‑‑‑‑‑‑‑‑‑‑‑‑‑‑‑‑‑‑‑‑‑

93 CB

If recommended by current charter member:

Name‑‑‑‑‑‑‑‑‑‑‑‑‑‑‑ NAFC No. ‑‑‑‑‑‑‑

BUSINESS REPLY CARD
FIRST CLASS   PERMIT NO. 1557   HOPKINS, MN

POSTAGE WILL BE PAID BY ADDRESSEE

North American Fishing Club
12301 Whitewater Dr.
P.O. Box 3405
Minnetonka, MN 55343

NO POSTAGE
NECESSARY
IF MAILED
IN THE
UNITED STATES

(tape or staple here)